Here we go again!
Vor dir liegt der Wordmaster.
Er hilft dir beim Wörterlernen.

Sobald du neue Wörter in der Schule besprochen hast, mach die **Words and phrases** in diesem Heft.

Die **fett gedruckten** deutschen Wörter und Ausdrücke sind Lernwörter. Sie fehlen im englischen Satz, damit du sie eintragen kannst.

Tipps:

1 Die Reihenfolge der Words and phrases entspricht der Reihenfolge der neuen Wörter im Vocabulary deines Schülerbuches. Dort kannst du deine Lösungen überprüfen.

2 Wenn du mal nicht weiter weißt, kannst du auch im Vocabulary nachschauen.

3 Lerne neue Wörter in einem Satz. So kannst du sie dir besser merken.

1 Words and phrases ➔ *(pp. 8–10)*

1 Where is our first _____?   Wo ist unser erster **Halt**?

2 We're going _____. Great!   Wir fahren **zelten**. Großartig!

3 This is the best place _____!   Das ist der schönste Ort **der Welt**.

4 It's _____ today.   Heute ist es **sonnig**.

Übrigens: Im Anschluss an die **Words and phrases** gibt es kurze Aufgaben, Rätsel und Wortspiele, mit denen du den neuen Wortschatz weiter üben und festigen kannst.

Alle Lösungen findest du in der Mitte des Heftes.

In the holidays

1 Words and phrases → (pp. 8–10)

1 Where is our first _____?	Wo ist unser erster **Halt**?
2 We're going _____. Great!	Wir fahren **zelten**. Großartig!
3 This is the best place _____!	Das ist der schönste Ort **der Welt**.
4 It's _____ today.	Heute ist es **sonnig**.
5 The _____ are _____.	Die **Berge** sind **schön**.
6 I'm not _____. I'm here with Mark.	Ich bin nicht **allein**. Ich bin mit Mark hier.
7 Please _____.	**Grüß ihn** bitte **von mir**.
8 The _____ are really big.	Die **Wellen** sind wirklich groß.
9 The _____ isn't nice: it's _____.	Das **Wetter** ist nicht schön: Es ist **bewölkt**.
10 Their _____ is near the _____.	Ihr **Wohnwagen** steht in der Nähe des **Vergnügungsparks**.
11 It's too _____. We can't do the _____.	Es ist zu **windig**. Wir können das **Projekt** nicht machen.
12 _____ to see you.	**Ich kann es kaum erwarten**, dich zu sehen.
13 In the _____ there's a lot of _____.	Im **Regenwald** gibt es viel **Regen**.
14 So the _____ are so green.	Deshalb sind die **Pflanzen** so grün.
15 There's a _____ for you.	Es gibt eine **Nachricht** für dich.

2 Match the parts

Ordne die Satzanfänge 1–6 den Satzenden a–f zu.

1 This park is my favourite place …

2 When you see Jon, say hello to him …

3 We can't wait to go …

4 There are so many plants. It's very green …

5 I think there's a message …

6 I'm not alone. I'm here …

a … on holiday.

b … with friends.

c … in the world.

d … from me.

e … for you.

f … in the rainforest.

3 Words and phrases ➜ (pp. 10–13)

1 There was a _____ for you.	Es gab einen **Anruf** für dich.
2 I _____ _____ _____. I was ____.	Ich **bin ans Telefon gegangen**. Ich war **zu Hause**.
3 You were _____. He _____ ___ _____.	Du warst **nicht da**. Er **hat eine Nachricht hinterlassen**.
4 You were _____ …	Du warst **in Urlaub** …
5 _____?	**Wie war es**?
6 It was cold _____ so we had a _____.	**Anfangs** war es kalt, und deshalb hatten wir ein **Rennen**.
7 It was my first holiday in a different _____.	Es war mein erster Urlaub in einem anderen **Land**.
8 The _____ are different too.	Auch die **Gebäude** sind anders.
9 _____ I can _____ my photos.	**Morgen** kann ich meine Fotos **mitbringen**.
10 ____ you want, you can look at them.	**Wenn** du willst, kannst du sie dir anschauen.
11 This exercise is a _____ of verbs.	Diese Aufgabe ist eine **Wiederholung** von Verben.
12 I need a pen. _____.	Ich brauche einen Stift. **Bleiben Sie am Apparat**.
13 _____ on a _____.	**Mache Notizen** auf deinem **Spickzettel**.

4 Scrambled words

Die Buchstaben sind durcheinandergeraten. Schreibe die Wörter richtig auf.

1 I made lots of **stone** in class.   _____

2 The **ertawhe** was very **yndiw**.   _____ _____

3 You were **uto** so I **eftl** a **samgese**.   _____ _____ _____

4 **thaw** is a **diohaly elik** in a **varaanc**?   _____ _____ _____ _____

5 Missing letters

Welche Buchstaben fehlen? Schreib sie in die Lücken. Sie ergeben von oben nach unten gelesen ein neues Wort.

1 The__e's a __evision class tomo__ __ow.

2 I l__ke camp__ng __n the mounta__ns.

3 Please brin__ a __ood book to the buildin__.

4 __old on __ere a minute, please.

5 Please __ell me where our firs__ s__op is.

6 Words and phrases ➔ (p. 14)

1 Our _____ is called Mrs Smith.	Unsere **Nachbarin** heißt Mrs Smith.
2 She had _____ with us.	Sie hatte **eine leichte Nachmittagsmahlzeit** mit uns.
3 At end of the note was "_____, Mum".	Am Ende der Notiz stand „**Liebe Grüße**, Mama".
4 Do they know? _____?	Wissen sie Bescheid? **Wem hast du es erzählt**?
5 _____ _____ Leo _____? He's new here.	**Wen kennt** Leo? Er ist neu hier.
6 I like lots of things, sports _____.	Ich mag viele Sachen, **zum Beispiel** Sport.
7 I had a nice _____ today.	Ich hatte heute eine nette **Überraschung**.
8 It was late, but they _____ didn't go to bed.	Es war spät, aber sie gingen **trotzdem** nicht ins Bett.
9 Let's go to the library _____.	Lass uns **heute Nachmittag** zur Bibliothek gehen.
10 Leo _____ _____ Plymstock two weeks ago.	Leo **ist** vor zwei Wochen **nach** Plymstock **umgezogen**.
11 The Blackwells have two _____ and a _____.	Die Blackwells haben zwei **Söhne** und eine **Tochter**.
12 Do the Coopers _____ know many people here?	Kennen die Coopers **schon** viele Leute hier?
13 Yes, I'm _____ they know lots of people.	Ja, ich bin **sicher**, dass sie viele Leute kennen.
14 They _____ us to dinner today.	Sie **haben** uns heute zum Abendessen **eingeladen**.
15 Do you _____ invite people to your house?	Lädst du **jemals** Leute zu dir nach Hause ein?

7 Word snake

Suche Wörter in der Wortschlange und trage sie in die Sätze ein.

movemovedsurprisesurprisedinviteinvitedthinkcomeliked

1 We … to Plymouth from London last year. _____

2 My parents … some friends to visit us. _____

3 It was a nice … to see you this morning. _____

8 True or false?

	True	False		True	False
1 Your neighbour lives near you.	◯	◯	3 "This afternoon" is the same as "tomorrow".	◯	◯
2 You can eat tea in England.	◯	◯	4 Your sister is your mother's daughter.	◯	◯

9 Words and phrases → (pp. 15–17)

1 You can go to bed when you want? _____!	Du kannst ins Bett, wann du willst? **Du Glückspilz!**
2 I won the game. I _____ _____.	Ich habe das Spiel gewonnen. **Ich hatte Glück.**
3 I _____ my sister in the afternoon.	Nachmittags **passe** ich **auf** meine Schwester **auf.**
4 _____ you _____ to go to the park with her?	**Darfst** du mit ihr in den Park gehen?
5 How fast can you _____ a tennis ball?	Wie schnell kannst du einen Tennisball **schlagen?**
6 The ball _____ down the hill.	Der Ball **ist** den Hügel **hinuntergerollt.**
7 We went _____ because the weather was nice.	Wir gingen **nach draußen**, da das Wetter schön war.
8 Our team won a _____.	Unser Team hat einen **Preis** gewonnen.
9 You want it? _____.	Willst du es haben? **Bitte sehr.**
10 Today we have English, _____?	Heute haben wir Englisch, **nicht wahr?**
11 What does this word _____?	Was **bedeutet** dieses Wort?
12 *We like football – "We" is the _____.*	*Wir mögen Fußball – „Wir" ist das* **Subjekt.**
13 Right, and "football" is the _____.	Richtig, und „Fußball" ist das **Objekt.**

10 Word search

Finde die Wörter im Wortgitter →↓ und vervollständige mit ihnen die Sätze.

1 You're going to the USA? _____ you!

2 I _____ after my baby brother every Friday.

3 The ball _____ me on the nose. Ow!

4 Are you _____ to go to bed when you want?

5 There's no school. We're on _____.

6 _____ the ball to me.

7 My work was best, so I got a _____.

8 Do you _____ watch films in English?

9 Let's have a _____ from here to school.

10 I'm not _____ what this new word _____.

K	H	I	T	P	G	B	A
L	O	O	K	R	O	L	L
R	L	T	T	I	S	U	L
D	I	C	Y	Z	U	C	O
W	D	E	V	E	R	K	W
R	A	C	E	V	E	Y	E
I	Y	M	E	A	N	S	D

11 Words and phrases ➜ *(pp. 18–20)*

1 _____ with me when you arrive.	**Setz dich** mit mir **in Verbindung**, wenn du ankommst.
2 We can _____ by email.	Wir können per E-Mail **in Verbindung bleiben**.
3 No, send me a _____.	Nein, schicke mir eine **SMS**.
4 They're easy, but not _____.	Sie sind einfach, aber nicht **kostenlos**.
5 What do the school _____ say about mobiles?	Was steht in den Schul**regeln** über Handys?
6 I need to call my _____.	Ich muss meine **Gastfamilie** anrufen.
7 Guess the _____ from the _____.	Rate die **Bedeutung** aus dem **Zusammenhang**.
8 That man _____ be rich.	Der Mann da **muss** reich sein.
9 There's a _____ word in German.	Es gibt ein **ähnliches** Wort auf Deutsch.
10 The dog stopped but we walked ____.	Der Hund hielt an, aber wir gingen **weiter**.
11 He sings _____ his father.	Er singt **genau wie** sein Vater.
12 I _____ so _____.	Ich **habe mich** so **gelangweilt**.
13 Next _____ I'm at a _____.	Nächstes **Trimester** gehe ich auf ein **Internat**.
14 I wasn't bored. I was _____.	Ich habe mich nicht gelangweilt. Ich war **entsetzt**.
15 Some schools have nice _____ activities.	Manche Schulen haben schöne Aktivitäten **im Freien**.

12 Scrambled questions

Schreibe die Wörter in der richtigen Reihenfolge auf.
Dann beantworte die Fragen.

Yes   No

1 Do with every you friend get your in week touch?

   _____   ◯ ◯

2 day more you Do send 10 or text every messages?

   _____   ◯ ◯

3 school a your boarding Is school?

   _____   ◯ ◯

4 Can of example you an outdoor give an activity?

   _____   ◯ ◯

13 Words and phrases → (pp. 20–24)

1 We want to _____ this weekend.	Wir wollen dieses Wochenende **klettern**.
2 I'm _____ _____ ____ the holiday.	Ich **freue mich auf** den Urlaub.
3 I see _____. She must be _____.	Ich sehe **Tränen**. Sie muss **unglücklich** sein.
4 I don't want to talk about the _____.	Ich will nicht über die **Zukunft** sprechen.
5 It isn't cold. You don't need a _____ today.	Es ist nicht kalt. Du brauchst heute keine **Jacke**.
6 Put that in your _____ or in the _____.	Tu das in deine **Tasche** oder in den **Abfalleimer**.
7 Dad has an _____ in the USA.	Papa hat eine **Wohnung** in den USA.
8 The TV _____ is big and the _____ too!	Der TV-**Bildschirm** ist groß und die **Pommes** auch!
9 We _____ ____ _____ after dinner.	Wir **haben** nach dem Abendessen **abgewaschen**.
10 I went there ____ be with Dad.	Ich bin dort hingefahren, **um** bei Papa **zu** sein.
11 They _____ after 14 hours on the ship.	Sie **gingen an Land** nach 14 Stunden auf dem Schiff.
12 It was good to be on the _____ again.	Es war gut, wieder an **Land** zu sein.
13 What are you doing _____?	Was machst du **jetzt gerade**?
14 I'm _____ a _____.	Ich **bestelle** gerade einen **Pfannkuchen**.
15 This is a photo of me _____ the restaurant.	Das ist ein Foto von mir **vor** dem Restaurant.

14 Wrong! Wrong!

Finde in jedem Satz zwei Fehler und verbessere sie.

1 I'm climing a montain with my dad this weekend.   _____   _____

2 I'm really look forwad to our holiday.   _____   _____

3 Our appartment has a TV with a big screne.   _____   _____

4 We had pancaks and fries then watched the dishes.   _____   _____

5 It was cold so I wore my jaket when I went out side.   _____   _____

6 He wasn't unhapy when he thought about the futur.   _____   _____

15 Words and phrases → (pp. 24–25)

1 Our _____ is _____ a road.	Unser **Zeltplatz** ist **neben** einer Straße.
2 Our _____ is not very big.	Unser **Zelt** ist nicht sehr groß.
3 We climbed up the mountain. It was _____.	Wir sind auf den Berg geklettert. Er war **felsig**.
4 We watched the _____ of the clouds.	Wir beobachteten die **Schatten** der Wolken.
5 We made a big _____ in the evening.	Wir haben am Abend ein großes **Feuer** gemacht.
6 I _____ and watched the night _____.	Ich **schaute auf** und beobachtete den Nacht**himmel**.
7 Dad _____ when I came home.	Papa **hat geschlafen**, als ich nach Hause kam.
8 Take a _____ _____ we can see.	Nimm eine **Taschenlampe**, **damit** wir sehen können.
9 There are lots of _____ animals there.	Es gibt da viele **wilde** Tiere.
10 They came to our tent _____.	Sie kamen **immer wieder** zu unserem Zelt.
11 Dad _____ the torch.	Papa **hat** die Taschenlampe **ausgeschaltet**.
12 Then he _____ me a _____.	Dann **hat** er mich **umarmt**.
13 _____ I can make my _____ film.	**Dieses Mal** kann ich meinen **eigenen** Film machen.
14 I have fantastic _____ of the holiday.	Ich habe fantastische **Erinnerungen** an den Urlaub.

16 Broken words

Bilde Wörter, indem du die Teile miteinander verbindest, und vervollständige die Sätze.

1 Put that in the _____ bin.

2 Our tent is on a fantastic _____.

3 I'm reading my book and dad is _____.

4 Our mountain walk was hard because it was so _____.

5 I didn't know what to _____.

6 Our tent is in the _____ of that tree.

shad
lit
site
sleep
der
camp
ow
rock
or
y
a
ter

17 Crossword

Across →

2 The Beatles were a ▢▢▢ when my dad was a boy.

5 Today is the last day of my holiday. – I go home ▢▢▢ .

6 This is where you can see lots of animals.

8 If you find some money, you're ▢▢▢ .

10 There are no clouds. The ▢▢▢ is blue.

11 What does that word ▢▢▢ ?

12 Get ▢▢▢ touch with me when you are in England.

15 A ▢▢▢ school is a school where you sleep.

17 ▢▢▢ = water from the sky

18 Say hello ▢▢▢ Mark if you see him.

19 This year we went ▢▢▢ holiday to America.

20 We invited our neighbour to have ▢▢▢ with us.

22 I don't like this ▢▢▢ – it's rainy.

24 The mountains were so ▢▢▢ – I took lots of photos.

27 I am starting at a new school next ▢▢▢ .

29 After our holiday, let's stay in ▢▢▢ .

31 He wasn't in, so I left a ▢▢▢ .

32 ▢▢▢ = windig

34 I always send my grandma a ▢▢▢ from my holiday.

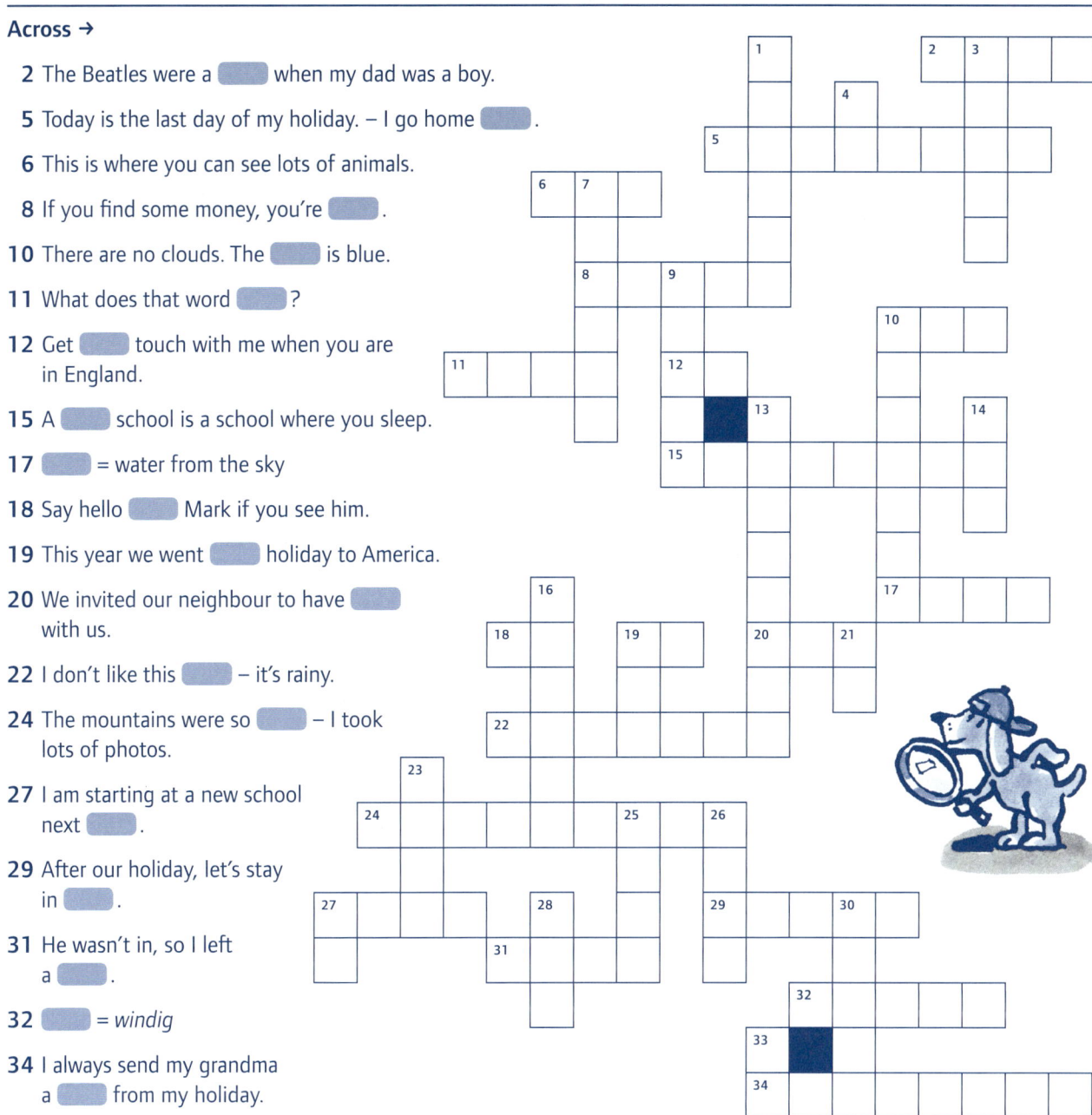

Down ↓

1 ▢▢▢ = bewölkt

3 I wasn't ▢▢▢ – I was with Dad.

4 There are lots of activities to ▢▢▢ here.

7 You can look for information ▢▢▢ or in a book.

9 I want to ▢▢▢ that mountain.

10 We say "project" in English. Do you have a ▢▢▢ word in German?

13 He has three sons and one ▢▢▢ .

14 The holiday started a week ▢▢▢ .

16 ▢▢▢ = a big group of trees

19 Is John at home, or he is ▢▢▢ ?

21 ▢▢▢ first I thought you were American.

23 She was unhappy – I saw a ▢▢▢ in her eye.

25 You don't have to buy it – it's ▢▢▢ .

26 Hurry! I don't want to be ▢▢▢ for school.

27 I'm looking forward ▢▢▢ seeing you again.

28 Sally is their daughter, and Henry is their ▢▢▢ .

30 ▢▢▢ = Pommes frites

33 I looked ▢▢▢ to the top of the mountain.

A school day

1 Words and phrases → *(pp. 28–29)*

1 We have a _____ club after school.	Wir haben einen **Schauspiel**klub nach der Schule.
2 _____ musical is *Grease*.	Das **diesjährige** Musical ist *Grease*.
3 _____ was *West Side Story*.	Das **vom letzten Jahr** war *West Side Story*.
4 The _____ is tomorrow.	Das **Vorsingen** ist morgen.
5 That's where _____ _____.	Da **singen** die **Sängerinnen**.
6 And the _____ _____.	Und die **Tänzer tanzen**.
7 Usually you have to _____ for that.	Normalerweise muss man dafür **Schlange stehen**.
8 My phone _____ in the cinema!	Mein Handy **hat** im Kino **geklingelt**!
9 My teacher _____ my name.	Mein Lehrer **rief** meinen Namen **auf**.
10 Look, there's an _____ about our school.	Schau mal, da ist ein **Artikel** über unsere Schule.

2 Scrambled questions

Die Wörter sind durcheinandergeraten. Ordner sie und schreibe die Fragen richtig auf.

1 drama you school Do have at lessons?

_____

_____

2 a to club auditions join Are football there?

_____

_____

3 queue to you to Do have tickets buy cinema?

_____

_____

4 have you lunch for yesterday Did pizza?

_____

_____

5 dancer a you good or Are singer?

_____

_____

6 phone many your did times yesterday How ring?

_____

_____

3 Words and phrases → (pp. 30–31)

1 I've got my _____ in. I can't hear you.	Ich habe meine **Ohrhörer** drin. Ich kann dich nicht hören.
2 Today we _____ write a story in class.	Heute **werden** wir im Unterricht eine Geschichte schreiben.
3 It _____ be an interesting lesson.	Es **wird** eine interessante Stunde sein.
4 This song is ____ my favourite singer.	Dieses Lied ist **von** meinem Lieblingssänger.
5 I wasn't _____. Well, _____.	Ich war nicht **nervös**. Naja, **ein bisschen** schon.
6 You dance well. You _____ join the club.	Du tanzt gut. Du **solltest** in einen Klub eintreten.
7 Who is that on the other _____ of the road?	Wer ist das auf der anderen Straßen**seite**?
8 I have _____ good friends here.	Ich habe hier **ein paar** gute Freunde.
9 "I sing" is the _____; "I sang" is the past.	„I sing" ist die **Gegenwart**; „I sang" ist die Vergangenheit.
10 We're _____ write a _____.	Wir **haben vor**, einen **Dialog** zu schreiben.

4 Missing words

Welche Präpositionen fehlen? Trage sie in die Lücken ein.

1 Don't be late _____ the lesson – it starts ____ five minutes.

2 The students queue ____ front ____ the class till the teacher gets there.

3 What do you normally have _____ lunch ____ Monday?

4 We have to write an article _____ music _____ homework.

5 They talked about their plans ____ the way ____ school.

5 Broken words

Bilde Wörter, indem du die Wortteile miteinander verbindest, und vervollständige die Sätze.

1 It's a _____ with two speakers.

2 He can't hear. He's got his _____ in his ears.

3 I'm not _____ about the test. I did lots of revision.

4 The _____ for the school show are today.

5 We're doing the _____ _Grease_ this time.

6 Words and phrases → (p. 32)

1 It's late. I'm _____ _____ _____ bed.	Es ist spät. Ich **mache mich fürs** Bett **fertig**.
2 You have your book, but where's _____?	Du hast dein Buch, aber wo ist **meins**?
3 The teacher gave us the _____.	Der Lehrer hat uns das **Arbeitsblatt** gegeben.
4 Which is the _____ river in Germany?	Welcher ist der **längste** Fluss Deutschlands?
5 We have to _____ the map.	Wir müssen die Karte **beschriften**.
6 There was an old _____ on the _____ bottle.	Es gab ein altes **Etikett** auf der **größten** Flasche.
7 I'm _____ well with the exercise.	Ich **komme** mit der Übung **gut voran**.
8 Do you _____ the exercise is too easy?	**Willst** du damit **sagen**, dass die Übung zu einfach ist?
9 Well, it's _____ ____ difficult ____ other exercises.	Nein, sie ist **nicht so** schwierig **wie** andere Übungen.
10 I think it's easier _____ the last exercise.	Ich denke, sie ist einfacher **als** die letzte Übung.
11 I'm going to _____ some new shoes today.	Ich werde mir heute neue Schuhe **besorgen**.
12 I _____ angry when he said that.	Ich **wurde** böse, als er das sagte.
13 I like your picture. _____ is _____.	Ich mag dein Bild. **Unseres** ist **schrecklich**.

7 The right words

Vervollständige die Sätze mit den richtigen Wörtern.

1   This pizza is _____ good. It's better _____ I thought.

2   I don't feel ____ nervous ____ last year. That was awful!

3   The rivers in England are _____ but there are _____ rivers in America.

4   The exercises yesterday were _____ _____ the examples we did in class today.

5   You can find _____ lakes _____ Loch Ness in other countries.

6   Yes, Loch Ness is _____ the _____ but it is big.

larger · than

longer · than

very · than

as · as

long · longer

not · largest

8 Words and phrases → (pp. 33–35)

1 I made a _____.	Ich habe einen **Fehler** gemacht.
2 How big is Malta? – 316 _____ _____.	Wie groß ist Malta? – 316 **Quadratkilometer**.
3 How _____ are you? And how _____ is your family?	Wie **groß** bist du? Und wie **groß** ist deine Familie?
4 Which is the longest river ____ _____?	Welcher Fluss ist der längste **auf der Erde**?
5 I think he's _____ as fast as you.	Ich denke, er ist **ungefähr** so schnell wie du.
6 But he's not as fast as a _____!	Aber er ist nicht so schnell wie ein **Flugzeug**!
7 We sometimes _____ in class.	Manchmal **lesen** wir im Unterricht **laut vor**.
8 _____ you call him.	**Achte darauf**, dass du ihn anrufst.
9 I have _____ here in my bag.	Ich habe **alles** hier in meiner Tasche.
10 He _____ before he answered.	Er **legte eine Pause ein**, bevor er antwortete.
11 The film was scary – I _____ _____.	Der Film war gruselig – ich **hatte Angst**.
12 _____ is important.	Die **Zeichensetzung** ist wichtig.
13 He saw his mistake and _____ his answer.	Er sah seinen Fehler und **änderte** seine Antwort.

9 Word search

Finde die fehlenden Wörter → ↓ im Buchstabengitter und vervollständige die Sätze.

1 'Loch' _____ lake. It's a word that they use in _____.

2 Please read _____ so we can all hear.

3 That isn't right. It's a _____.

4 I wasn't as _____ as I thought.

5 We have to _____ all the rivers on the map.

6 You can't swim from here to America, but you can go by _____.

7 That's not your book. It's _____ so can I have it, please?

8 How _____ is the mountain?

F	J	A	W	W	Z	E	S
L	H	A	L	O	U	D	C
G	S	C	A	R	E	D	O
G	K	L	L	K	I	L	T
M	E	A	N	S	L	M	L
F	H	I	G	H	S	I	A
M	L	A	B	E	L	N	N
P	L	A	N	E	M	E	D
N	M	I	S	T	A	K	E

I have to write the answer on the ◯◯◯◯◯◯◯◯◯.

10 Words and phrases → (pp. 36–37)

1 He's a good singer, but he's not _____.	Er ist ein guter Sänger, aber er ist nicht **großartig**.
2 This is my favourite song. What's _____?	Das ist mein Lieblingslied. Was ist **deins**?
3 My picture is ok, but _____ is _____.	Mein Bild ist OK, aber **ihres** ist **herrlich**.
4 And _____ is _____ _____ beautiful.	Und **seins** ist **sogar noch** schöner.
5 I think it's the _____ interesting picture here.	Ich denke, es ist das interessant**este** Bild hier.
6 Well, it's the best _____.	Naja, es ist das beste **bis jetzt**.
7 I went ____ _____ to sing.	Ich bin **auf die Bühne** gegangen, um zu singen.
8 I was there _____.	Ich war **alleine** da.
9 We watched the _____ singers.	Wir haben die **begabten** Sänger beobachtet.
10 Then we _____ and _____.	Dann **haben** wir **gejubelt** und **geklatscht**.

11 The best words

Vervollständige die Sätze, indem du passende Wörter aus den Zetteln auswählst.

1 Today is the hottest day _____ this year.

2 I think that's a good idea, but this idea is _____ better.

3 Which is the _____ interesting place you know?

4 I know my mobile number. Do you know _____?

5 My name is Henry, and _____ is Jane.

1 so long · so far · so much · so often

2 more · ever · even · very

3 more · best · most · so

4 you · yours · your · you're

5 mine · his · hers · your

12 Odd one out

Kreise in jeder Gruppe das Wort ein, das nicht zu den anderen passt.

1 brilliant   talented   great   easy   _____

2 pause   move   wait   stop   _____

3 river   lake   see   loch   _____

4 ring   think   sing   clap   _____

5 question   mistake   wrong   problem   _____

13 Words and phrases ➜ (pp. 38–39)

1 We're going to the _____ this evening.	Wir gehen heute Abend ins **Theater**.
2 Then there's a _____ tomorrow.	Und morgen gibt es ein **Konzert**.
3 I hope someone is playing the _____.	Ich hoffe, dass jemand **Blockflöte** spielt.
4 How many _____ are there in "beautiful"?	Wie viele **Silben** gibt es im Wort „beautiful"?
5 I like _____. It's interesting.	Ich mag **Mode**. Sie ist interessant.
6 I want to travel _____ the world after school.	Nach der Schule will ich **um die** Welt reisen.
7 Where's the _____, please?	Wo ist bitte das **Rathaus**?
8 This is a photo of me in the _____!	Das ist ein Foto von mir im **Schnee**.
9 _____ dog is that?	**Wessen** Hund ist das?
10 My cat sits with its _____ on the _____.	Meine Katze sitzt mit ihren **Pfoten** auf der **Treppe**.

14 Scrambled story

Verbinde die Texte **A** (Anfang) bis **J** (Ende) so, dass sie eine Geschichte ergeben.

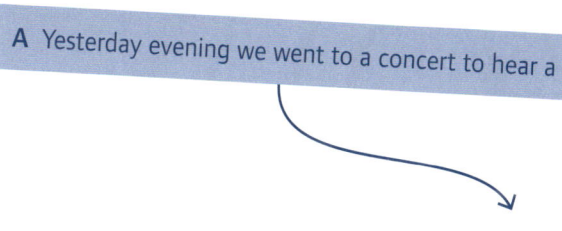

A Yesterday evening we went to a concert to hear a

I brilliant. I knew almost all the songs, and can play one

E as I thought. Tonight I am doing something

D songs from great musicals. I really liked it. It was

G or two on my recorder. They are not as difficult

B show, because my friends and I like

C different: I am going into town to see a fashion

F group of very talented young singers. They sang

J hall, and the best thing is that it's free!

H clothes. We're all going to be designers or models. It's in the town

Answer:

15 Words and phrases ➜ (pp. 40–41)

1 I like your poster, but it _____ be better.	Ich mag dein Poster, aber es **könnte** besser sein.
2 But I think the text is very _____.	Ich denke aber, dass der Text sehr **deutlich** ist.
3 Are you happy with the _____ of the pictures?	Bist du glücklich mit der **Größe** der Bilder?
4 I made sure all the words are _____.	Ich habe darauf geachtet, dass alle Wörter **richtig** sind.
5 Next time, we could do it _____.	Nächstes Mal könnten wir es **so** machen.
6 The teacher said we should _____ on the floor.	Der Lehrer sagte, wir sollten auf dem Fußboden **liegen**.
7 A photo of us: we _____ on the floor.	Ein Bild von uns: Wir **liegen** auf dem Boden.
8 Please can you _____ me _____ very early?	Kannst du mich bitte sehr früh **wecken**?
9 When I sing on stage, I feel very _____.	Wenn ich auf der Bühne singe, bin ich sehr **schüchtern**.

16 Missing words

Vervollständige den Text mit Wörtern aus der Wortschlange.

1 Today we worked in _____ and made _____ in class.

2 _____ was very _____, I think.

3 We made _____ there were no _____

4 in the _____, and that the _____ were

5 _____. The teacher said it was very _____

6 and asked what _____ be _____. I said

7 that I thought we could use _____ _____

8 and make the poster a _____ _____ next time.

17 Words and phrases → (p. 42)

→ (p. 42)

1 She _____ her money into her pocket.	Sie **steckte** ihr Geld in ihre Tasche.
2 You can't eat soup with a _____!	Du kannst Suppe nicht mit einer **Gabel** essen!
3 It's silly to use a _____, too.	Es ist auch albern, ein **Messer** zu benutzen.
4 That's better! It's easier to eat with a _____.	Das ist besser! Es ist einfacher, mit einem **Löffel** zu essen.
5 Don't _____ the camera. It's expensive.	**Lass** die Kamera nicht **fallen**, sie ist teuer.
6 Do you put _____ in your hair?	Tust du **Gel** in deine Haare?
7 I'm going to need my _____ today.	Ich werde heute meine **Sonnenbrille** brauchen.
8 My dad doesn't wear _____.	Mein Vater trägt keine **Brille**.
9 You should move your _____ when you dance.	Du solltest deine **Arme** bewegen, wenn du tanzt.
10 If you _____ your head it means "no".	Wenn du den Kopf **schüttelst**, bedeutet das „nein".

18 Q & A

Welche Fragen und Antworten passen zusammen? Ordne sie einander richtig zu.

1 What are you doing tonight?

2 What about you? Are you coming, too?

3 What are you going to wear?

4 Is your sister the best singer in your family?

5 Why are you clapping?

6 He's got gel in his hair.

7 Can you stick my camera in your bag?

8 Great – this is my favourite song.

a I like the music.

b Let's dance, then.

c I'm going to the disco with my friends.

d Me, too.

e No, I can't. I have to stay at home.

f I don't want to drop it.

g I think I am better, actually.

h My new jeans and a T-shirt.

19 Punctuation

Schreibe die Satzzeichen als Wort.

 [ˌfʊl ˈstɒp] _____

[ˈkwestʃən mɑːk] _____

 [ˈkɒmə] _____

[ˌekskləˈmeɪʃn mɑːk] _____

 [ˈkəʊlən] _____

[ˈhaɪfən] _____

20 Words and phrases → (pp. 42–43)

1 Something _____. Was it your phone?	Etwas hat **gepiept**. War das dein Handy?
2 I _____ I _____ with my friends now.	Ich **wünschte**, ich **wäre** jetzt bei meinen Freunden.
3 I don't dance. I just _____ at the wall.	Ich tanze nicht. Ich **stelle mich** bloß an der Wand **hin**.
4 _____ _____ my friends like music.	**Die meisten von** meinen Freunden mögen Musik.
5 Answer the questions _____.	Beantworte die Fragen **eine nach der anderen**.
6 They are all easy, _____ one.	Sie sind alle einfach, **außer** der einen.
7 Who is that _____ boy?	Wer ist der **gutaussehende** Junge?
8 I don't know. _____, let's go home now.	Ich weiß es nicht. **Aber egal**, lass uns nach Hause gehen.

21 That's wrong!

Finde in jedem Satz einen Fehler und verbessere ihn.

1 I wish I am at the disco with you and not at home. _____

2 I think most of people like music. _____

3 We are geting ready to go to school. _____

4 I ring you on your mobile two hours ago. _____

5 It's a hot day. I'm going to wear my sunglass. _____

6 Who camera is this? It looks expensive. _____

7 I have to stay at home. Any way, I don't like discos. _____

8 Most of my friends are here, exept Greg. _____

9 Careful, don't let fall the camera. _____

10 How many silbles are there in "theatre"? _____

11 I read an interesting artikel in the paper. _____

12 Is this korrekt? It looks wrong. _____

13 We claped at the end of the concert. _____

14 Are you nervos when you speak in class? _____

15 I need to lable the map. _____

Wrong!

3 Unit

Out and about

1 Words and phrases → (pp. 46–47)

1 I was _____ every day last week.	Letzte Woche war ich jeden Tag **unterwegs**.
2 We live _____ the _____.	Wir wohnen **gegenüber von** der **Post**.
3 The _____ is next to a _____.	Der **Bahnhof** ist neben einer **Kirche**.
4 It's _____ of Castle St and Beach Rd.	Er ist auf der Castle Street, **Ecke** Beach Road.
5 Be careful when you _____ the road.	Sei vorsichtig, wenn du die Straße **überquerst**.
6 At the end of the road, _____.	**Biege** am Ende der Straße **nach rechts ab**.
7 The cinema is _____.	Das Kino ist **links**.
8 Go _____, _____ the school.	Geh **geradeaus weiter**, an der Schule **vorbei**.
9 _____, do you live here?	**Entschuldigen Sie**, wohnen Sie hier?
10 Can you _____ to the beach?	Können Sie **mir den Weg** zum Strand **beschreiben**?
11 Why did that man _____ you _____?	Warum hat der Mann dich **nach dem Weg gefragt**?
12 He isn't from here. He's a _____.	Er ist nicht von hier. Er ist ein **Besucher**.

2 In town

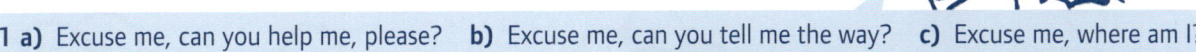

Bilde einen Dialog. Wähle dazu den passenden Satz in jeder Zeile aus.

1 a) Excuse me, can you help me, please?   b) Excuse me, can you tell me the way?   c) Excuse me, where am I?

2 a) Are you sure?   b) Of course you can.   c) Sure.

3 a) Are you near a post office?   b) Where is the train station?   c) Where are you from?

4 a) Turn left at the end of the road.   b) I'm out and about.   c) The cinema is opposite.

5 a) Right, and then left, OK.   b) I see, left at the end. Right.   c) OK, that's right.

6 a) Go past the train station.   b) On the left there are visitors.   c) Then go straight on.

7 a) Be careful when you cross the road.   b) Do I cross the road?   c) Is there a place to cross?

8 a) No, it's on the corner.   b) No, it's opposite.   c) No, it's not there.

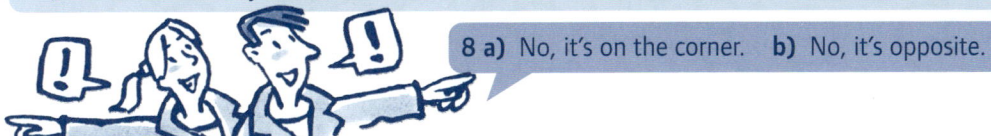

3 Words and phrases ➜ (pp. 48–49)

1 There are no cars in the _____.   Es gibt keine Autos in der **Fußgängerzone**.

2 Where were you _____ you left the shop?   Wo warst du, **nachdem** du den Laden verlassen hast?

3 It got cold _____ we got to the park.   Es wurde kalt, **gleich nachdem** wir den Park erreichten.

4 How much does a good computer _____?   Was **kostet** ein guter Computer?

5 The shops _____ now.   Die Geschäfte **schließen** jetzt.

6 Where can you buy _____ here?   Wo kann man hier **Pralinen** kaufen?

7 I _____ to buy _____ from a _____.   Ich **muss Blumen** von einem **Stand** kaufen.

8 We're in the _____ to see friends.   Wir sind in der **Stadt**, um Freunde zu besuchen.

9 I bought a _____ ruler and 12 _____.   Ich kaufte ein **Kunststoff**lineal und 12 **Filzstifte**.

10 My mobile rang ____ I was at the _____.   Mein Handy klingelte, **als** ich an der **Kasse** stand.

11 I paid the _____ for the ____.   Ich zahlte die **Verkäuferin** für den **Satz**.

12 H_____ you _____ everything now?   **Hast** du jetzt alles?

13 She gave me the _____. It was 2 p.   Sie gab mir das **Wechselgeld**. Es waren 2 Pence.

4 Broken words

Vervollständigen die Sätze, indem du Wörter mit den Wortteilen aus dem Rätsel bildest.

1 This is a _____ zone.

2 These _____ smell nice. They're beautiful, too.

3 I asked the shop _____ for help.

4 I bought some nice _____.

5 She gave me £5.20 _____.

6 At the weekend there are lots of _____.

7 We live _____ the station.

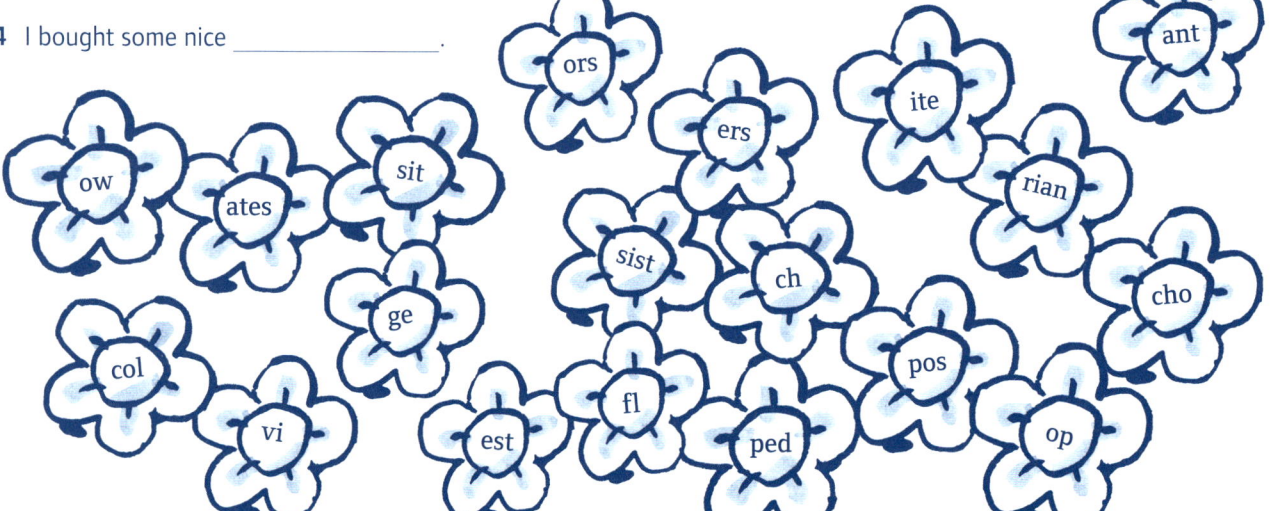

5 Words and phrases → (pp. 50–53)

1 Ask Grandma – she _____ _____ food.	Frag Oma – sie **kennt sich mit** Essen **aus**.
2 Please buy 250 _____ ____ butter,	Kauf bitte 250 **Gramm** Butter,
3 ... two _____ ____ biscuits,	... zwei **Packungen** Kekse,
4 ... a _____ ____ _____ , a _____ ____ _____ ,	... eine **Dose Suppe**, eine **Flasche Saft**,
5 ... and maybe _____ juice if you want.	... und vielleicht **Tomaten**saft, wenn du willst.
6 Yesterday I ate three _____ ____ _____ !	Gestern habe ich drei **Teller Pommes** gegessen!
7 Three _____ ____ oranges is better, you know.	Drei **Kilo** Orangen sind besser, weißt du.
8 We have a _____ ____ _____ in the kitchen.	Wir haben in der Küche einen **Obstkorb**.
9 I found a _____ there last week!	Letzte Woche habe ich da eine **Socke** gefunden!
10 Please _____ the text for names.	**Suche** bitte den Text **schnell** nach Namen **ab**.
11 This is a _____ from Paris.	Das ist ein **Andenken** aus Paris.

6 The right words

Vervollständige die Sätze mit den richtigen Wörtern aus den Keksen.

1 Are you _____? Let's open a _____ of biscuits.

2 Can I have some orange _____ to _____?

3 I need to buy 500 _____ of _____.

4 There's a big _____ of fruit on the _____.

5 I had a _____ of _____ for lunch.

6 This shop sells _____ for _____.

7 When you _____ a _____, you read quickly.

8 What did you do _____ you got _____?

9 There are lots of _____ in the _____.

10 How _____ is a _____ of oranges?

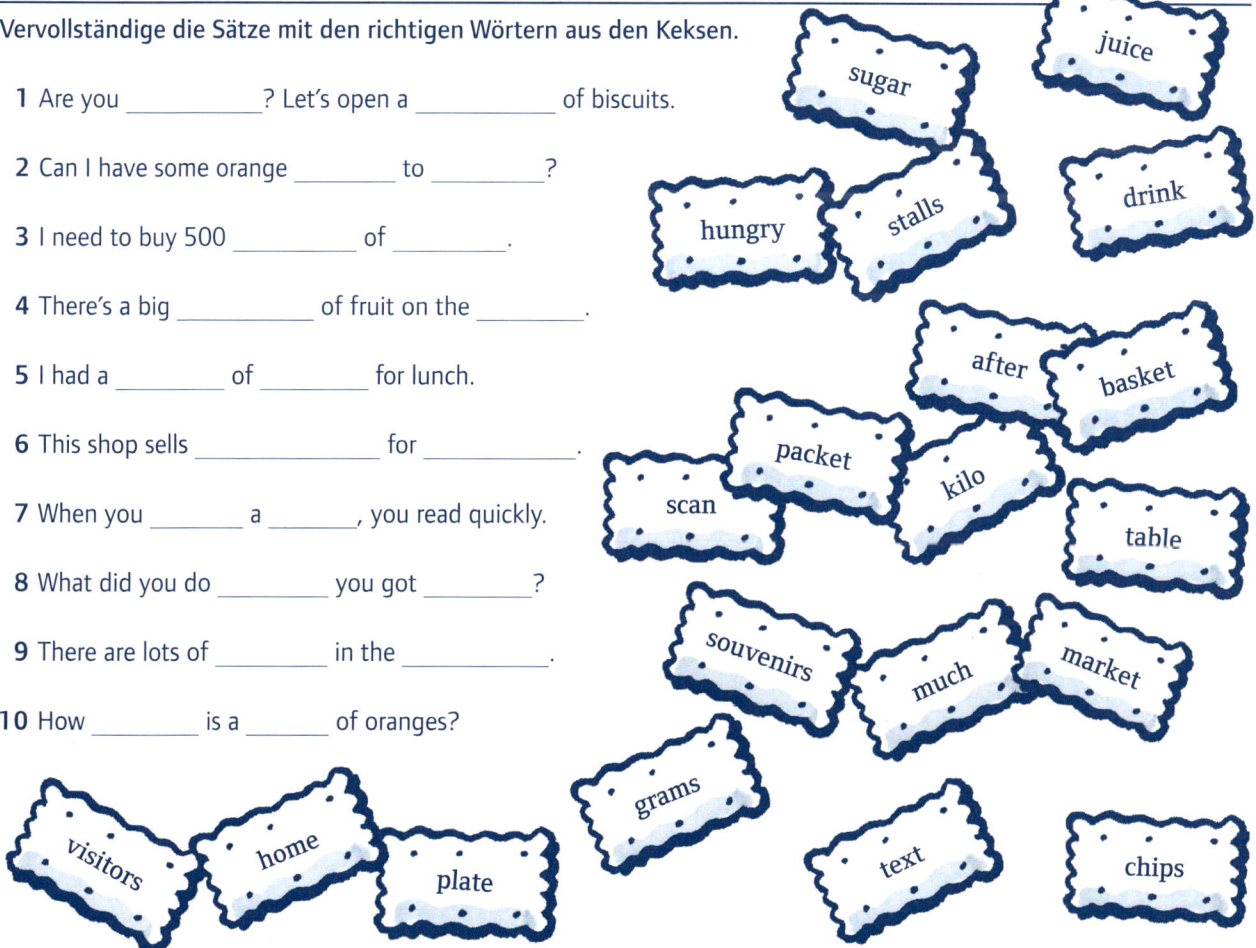

sugar · juice · hungry · stalls · drink · after · basket · packet · kilo · scan · table · souvenirs · much · market · grams · text · chips · visitors · home · plate

7 Words and phrases ➜ (p. 54)

1 I'm going to do a _____ trick for you.	Ich werde euch einen **Zauber**trick vorführen.
2 This idea could _____ us very rich people!	Diese Idee könnte uns **zu** sehr reichen Leuten **machen**!
3 In the film he _____ someone in the park.	Im Film **kämpft** er **gegen** jemanden im Park.
4 I went out. _____ it started to rain.	Ich ging raus. **Genau in dem Moment** fing es an zu regnen.
5 It's raining. Please ride my bike _____.	Es regnet. Fahr bitte **langsam** mit meinem Rad.
6 Let's climb that _____. It's not difficult.	Lass uns auf die **Mauer** klettern. Das ist nicht schwer.
7 He said "No!" _____.	Er sagte **mit lauter Stimme** „Nein".
8 You can go, but you must be _____.	Du kannst gehen, aber du musst **brav** sein.
9 I'm _____ for Dad's camera.	Ich bin für Papas Fotoapparat v**erantwortlich**.
10 He's a good dancer and he sings _____, too.	Er ist ein guter Tänzer und er singt auch **gut**.
11 We aren't late. _____.	Wir sind nicht zu spät. **Mach dir keine Sorgen**.
12 You look sad. What _____?	Du siehst traurig aus. Was **ist passiert**?

8 The best word

Vervollständige die Sätze mit dem richtigen Wort aus den Notizzetteln.

1 When Mum's angry, she talks ____ a loud voice.

with · on · by · in

at · now · just · so

2 The film started and _____ then my phone rang.

good · well · best · brave

3 I want you to be very _____, please.

4 My English isn't very good. Please speak _____.

slow · fast · slowly · quickly

5 Ask the teacher. She knows a lot _____ the city.

from · about · over · on

9 Opposites

Vervollständige die Gegensätze.

1 Close – o_____n

2 right – l____t

3 different – s_____r

4 awful – b_____t

5 sunny – r_____y

6 small – t___l

7 buy – s___l

8 subject – o_____t

9 mine – y_____s

10 Words and phrases ➜ (pp. 55–56)

1 Can you _____ the picture, please?	Kannst du bitte das Bild **beschreiben**?
2 "Come" and "go" are _____ verbs.	„Kommen" und „gehen" sind **unregelmäßige** Verben.
3 Choose an interesting _____ for your poster.	Wähle ein interessantes **Thema** für dein Poster aus.
4 Then we can _____ the posters on the wall.	Dann können wir die Poster an die Wand **hängen**.
5 I use red to _____ important things.	Ich verwende rot, um wichtige Sachen **hervorzuheben**.
6 I sometimes _____ some words.	Ich **unterstreiche** manchmal einige Wörter.
7 I made five different _____!	Ich habe fünf verschiedene **Entwürfe** gemacht.

11 Scrambled story

Verbinde die Texte **A** (Anfang) bis **M** (Ende) so, dass sie eine Geschichte ergeben.

A Last week we had a very interesting

E there were no mistakes with irregular

I who wanted to make a film. Then our

G teacher told us that we could make a

D lesson at school. It was in our English

B poster in English to describe the topic

C verbs, for example. She wanted us to

F we underlined some words. Then we hung

H highlight the important information, so

J of the story. She told us to write a

L draft of our ideas first, then to check that

K class. First, we read a story about some children

M it on the wall for everyone to read.

Answer: A ◯ ◯ ◯ ◯ ◯ ◯ ◯ ◯ ◯ ◯ M

12 Words and phrases ➔ (p. 58)

1 My mobile is _____. I need a new one.	Mein Handy ist **kaputt**. Ich brauche ein neues.
2 _____ I'm going shopping now.	**Deshalb** gehe ich jetzt einkaufen.
3 Don't open the _____.	Mach das **Tor** nicht auf.
4 He has an awful _____ on his finger.	Er hat einen schrecklichen **Schnitt** am Finger.
5 She _____ the picture out of the paper.	Sie hat das Bild aus der Zeitung **geschnitten**.
6 The rabbit _____. A good trick!	Das Kaninchen **ist verschwunden**. Ein guter Trick!
7 You _____! Come _____ to us!	Ihr **da unten**! Kommt zu uns **nach hier oben**!
8 I want to climb onto the _____ of the house.	Ich will auf das **Dach** unseres Hauses klettern.
9 I have a great _____ _____ the city from here.	Ich habe von hier einen großartigen **Blick auf** die Stadt.
10 Don't get in the boat. Stay on the _____.	Geh nicht aufs Boot. Bleib am **Ufer**.

13 Missing words

Vervollständige die Sätze, indem du zwei passende Wörter aus den Knochen auswählst.

1 The _____ in the park was _____.

2 That's _____ they climbed over _____.

3 They wanted to find a good _____ to make a _____.

4 For the first _____, one person _____ behind

5 the _____, then followed Sam _____.

6 The boy with the camera shouted _____ from the _____.

7 He had a great _____ from _____ there.

8 The second scene was a _____ by the _____.

9 They found an old _____ on the _____.

10 But the boat _____ before they were _____.

gate · ready · boat · view · hid · building · up · carefully · scene · Cut! · why · fight · broken · film · place · quietly · roof · lake · disappeared · shore

14 Words and phrases ➜ *(pp. 58–59)*

1 In the cinema, you should _____.	Im Kino solltest du **flüstern**.
2 It's not far from here, just a little _____.	Es ist nicht weit von hier, nur ein bisschen **weiter**.
3 Oh, no! I have a _____ in my pocket.	Ach nein! Ich habe ein **Loch** in meiner Tasche.
4 I went into the sea _____ my _____.	Ich bin **bis zur Taille** ins Meer gegangen.
5 The _____ way to get better is to practise.	**Der einzige** Weg, um besser zu werden, ist zu üben.
6 It looks like plastic, but it's _____.	Es sieht aus wie Plastik, ist aber **Holz**.
7 Come on! We're late! _____!	Na los! Wir sind spät dran! **Beeil dich**!
8 Our film was great _____ ____ your help.	Unser Film war großartig, **dank** deiner Hilfe.
9 It was so cold my _____ were blue.	Es war so kalt, dass meine **Lippen** blau waren.
10 I usually _____ my friends when I see them.	Meistens **umarme** ich meine Freunde, wenn ich sie sehe.
11 I climbed the tree and _____ my cat.	Ich kletterte auf den Baum und **rettete** meine Katze.

15 Scrambled dialogue

Verbinde die beiden Teile des Dialogs.

1 Why are you whispering?

2 How did Rocky get so wet?

3 What happened when you saw him?

4 Why are you nearly as wet as Rocky?

5 Your lips are blue.

6 OK, we can look for some new socks. Hurry!

a Yes, I'm very cold.

b I rescued him, of course.

c He fell in the river.

d I don't want Mum and Dad to hear us. That's why.

e Thanks. I can help you.

f Because there was a hole in the boat.

16 That's wrong!

Finde und verbessere einen Fehler in jeder Zeile.

1 Why did he dissapear? _____

2 He wispered because he wanted to be quiet. _____

3 The would of the boat was old. _____

4 They walked to the end of the road slow. _____

5 Please go and pay at the desk cash. _____

6 Have you a dog at home? _____

7 How much did your computer costed? It's great. _____

8 I don't want to be late. Hurry on! _____

10 There's a church just opposite of the school. _____

11 The film could get us famous! _____

17 Word search

Finde die fehlenden Wörter →↓↘↗ im Buchstabengitter und vervollständige die Sätze.

1 I was out and _____ all day yesterday.

2 He fell and now he has a _____ nose.

3 What time do shops _____ in the evening?

4 Be careful when you _____ the road.

5 I need a red _____ pen for my poster.

6 My shoes and _____ are wet.

7 You can _____ important words in yellow,

8 … or you can _____ them.

9 When you whisper, you talk in a quiet _____.

10 If you go away quickly, you _____.

11 Is your recorder plastic or _____?

12 Between the land and the sea is the _____.

13 You have a great _____ from tall buildings.

W	F	E	L	T	G	I	U	N	V	E	U
N	O	V	U	L	S	O	C	K	S	A	O
S	R	O	H	C	L	O	S	E	A	B	O
W	B	B	D	I	S	A	P	P	E	A	R
A	R	A	L	U	G	E	R	R	I	E	O
W	I	C	L	G	B	H	R	C	C	M	O
O	V	U	N	D	E	R	L	I	N	E	F
O	J	Y	F	R	G	O	O	I	Y	Y	H
D	C	R	O	S	S	V	O	K	G	B	K
T	O	H	A	E	O	I	E	Z	E	H	D
F	S	A	I	G	G	E	P	E	M	N	T
H	E	E	B	F	Q	W	K	E	W	U	H

18 -ing words

Vervollständige die -ing Wörter.

1 Please be quiet. The film is _____ing.

2 I think the topic is really _____ing.

3 I can't hear. They are _____ing.

4 Hurry up. The shops are _____ing.

5 That _____ing is the church.

6 The camera isn't _____ing.

7 I think your phone is _____ing.

8 He knows _____ing about the topic.

9 She's beautiful, and he's _____-_____ing, too.

10 There's no problem, so stop _____ing.

11 I hope you are _____ing better today.

12 They are _____ing a film in the park.

Welche vier Buchstaben des Alphabets werden in der Aufgabe nicht verwendet?

a b c d e f g h i j k l m n o p q r s t u v w x y z

19 24 x 5

Die Hinweise zeigen, wie die Wörter in der phonetischen Umschrift geschrieben werden.
Schreibe die Wörter in das Kreuzwortgitter. Alle 24 Wörter haben 5 Buchstaben.

Across →
1 [kʊd] 3 [ʃeɪk] 6 [stænd] 7 [raʊnd] 8 [ʃɔː] 10 [əˈləʊn] 11 [ˈhʌri] 14 [klaɪm]
15 [əˈbaʊt] 16 [ˈdrɑːmə] 18 [drɑːft] 19 [tɔːtʃ] 20 [ˈtɒpɪk] 21 [tʃɪə]

Down ↓
2 [ˈleɪbl] 3 [steɪdʒ] 4 [ɜːθ] 5 [ment] 6 [stʊd] 8 [stʌk]
9 [əˈlaʊd] 12 [faɪt] 13 [ˈmædʒɪk] 17 [ˈɑːftə]

On Dartmoor

1 Words and phrases ➜ (pp. 66–67)

1 Who is that in the _____? Ben?	Wer ist das im **Hintergrund**? Ben?
2 No, he's in the _____.	Nein, er ist im **Vordergrund**.
3 His name is _____ of the page.	Sein Name ist **am unteren Ende** der Seite.
4 I love the beautiful _____ in France.	Ich liebe die schöne **Landschaft** in Frankreich.
5 The lesson _____ with a test.	Die Stunde **fing** mit einem Test **an**.
6 They walked through the _____.	Sie liefen über die **Felder**.
7 You can see our _____ in the _____.	Du kannst unsere **Fußabdrücke** im **Gras** sehen.
8 How many _____ does a cow have?	Wie viele **Füße** hat eine Kuh?
9 I can't see much because of the _____.	Ich kann wegen des **Nebels** nicht so viele sehen.
10 We saw lots of _____ in the _____.	Wir sahen viele **Ponys** im **Tal**.
11 There were _____ and _____, too.	Es gab auch **Kühe** und **Schafe**.
12 Most farms have horses, _____, cows, _____.	Viele Bauernhöfe haben Pferde, **Ziegen**, Kühe **usw**.
13 We wrote a _____ about animals for homework.	Wir schrieben als Hausaufgabe ein **Gedicht** über Tiere.

2 Q & A

Ordne die Fragen 1–8 den richtigen Antworten a–h zu.

1 Can you see the house in the background?

2 Can you see the sheep over there?

3 What's that in the foreground in the picture?

4 Are those animals in the valley horses?

5 Where are the answers to the exercise?

6 Why don't you want to go in the field?

7 I think I can hear cows. Can you?

8 What do goats eat?

a No, I think they're ponies.

b Yes, they are in the valley, I think.

c At the bottom of the page, I think.

d I thought it was a school. It's very big.

e It's difficult because of the mist.

f Grass and things like that, I think.

g Because of the horses.

h I think it's the footprints of some animal.

Lösungen

1 Words and phrases

1 stop **2** camping **3** in the world
4 sunny **5** mountains; beautiful **6** alone
7 say hello to him for me **8** waves
9 weather; cloudy **10** caravan; fun park
11 windy; project **12** I can't wait
13 rainforest; rain **14** plants **15** message

2 Match the parts

1 c **2** d **3** a **4** f **5** e **6** b

3 Words and phrases

1 phone call **2** answered the phone; in
3 out; left a message **4** on holiday; What was it like?
5 at first; race **6** country **7** buildings
8 Tomorrow; bring **9** If **10** revision
11 Hold on a minute **12** Make notes; crib sheet

4 Scrambled words

1 notes **2** weather; windy **3** out; left; message
4 what; holiday; like; caravan

5 Missing letters

1 r **2** i **3** g **4** h **5** t
Das neue Wort: right

6 Words and phrases

1 neighbour **2** tea **3** Love **4** Who did you tell
5 Who; does; know **6** for example **7** surprise **8** still
9 this afternoon **10** moved to **11** sons; daughter
12 already **13** sure **14** invited **15** ever

7 Word snake

1 moved **2** invited **3** surprise

8 True or false?

1 True
2 True *(die ganze Mahlzeit wird "tea" genannt)*
3 False
4 True

9 Words and phrases

1 Lucky you! **2** was; lucky **3** look after **4** Are; allowed
5 hit **6** rolled **7** out **8** prize **9** Here you are
10 right **11** mean **12** subject **13** object

10 Word search

1 Lucky **2** look **3** hit **4** allowed **5** holiday
6 Roll **7** prize **8** ever **9** race **10** sure; means

11 Words and phrases

1 Get in touch with me **2** stay in touch **3** text message
4 free **5** rules **6** host family **7** meaning; context
8 must **9** similar **10** on **11** just like **12** was; bored
13 term; boarding school **14** shocked **15** outdoor

12 Scrambled questions

1 Do you get in touch with your friend every week?
2 Do you send 10 or more text messages every day?
3 Is your school a boarding school?
4 Can you give an example of an outdoor activity?

13 Words and phrases

1 climb **2** looking forward to **3** tears; unhappy
4 future **5** jacket **6** pocket; litter bin **7** apartment
8 screen; fries **9** washed the dishes **10** to **11** landed
12 land **13** right now **14** ordering; pancake
15 outside

1

14 Wrong! Wrong!

1 ~~climing~~ → climbing; ~~montain~~ → mountain
2 ~~look~~ → looking; ~~forwad~~ → forward
3 ~~appartment~~ → apartment; ~~screne~~ → screen
4 ~~pancaks~~ → pancakes; ~~watched~~ → washed
5 ~~jaket~~ → jacket; ~~out side~~ *(als zwei Wörter)* →
outside *(als eins)*
6 ~~unhapy~~ → unhappy; ~~futur~~ → future

15 Words and phrases

1 campsite; next to 2 tent 3 rocky 4 shadows 5 fire
6 looked up; sky 7 was asleep 8 torch; so that 9 wild
10 again and again 11 turned off 12 gave; hug
13 This time; own 14 memories

16 Broken words

1 litter 2 campsite 3 asleep 4 rocky 5 order
6 shadow

17 Crossword puzzle

Across: 2 band **5** tomorrow **6** zoo **8** lucky **10** sky
11 mean **12** in **15** boarding **17** rain **18** to **19** on
20 tea **22** weather **24** beautiful **27** term **29** touch
31 note **33** windy **35** postcard

Down: 1 cloudy **3** alone **4** do **7** online **9** climb
10 similar **13** daughter **14** ago **16** forest **19** out
21 at **23** tear **25** free **26** late **27** to **28** son
30 chips **32** by **34** up

Unit 2

1 Words and phrases

1 drama 2 This year's 3 Last year's 4 audition
5 singers; sing 6 dancers; dance 7 queue 8 rang
9 called out 10 article

2 Scrambled questions

1 Do you have drama lessons at school?
2 Are there auditions to join a football club?
3 Do you have to queue to buy cinema tickets?
4 Did you have pizza for lunch yesterday?
5 Are you a good singer or dancer?
6 How many times did your phone ring yesterday?

3 Words and phrases

1 earphones 2 are going to 3 is going to 4 by
5 nervous; a bit 6 You should 7 side 8 a few
9 present 10 going to; dialogue

4 Missing words

1 for; in 2 in; of 3 for; on 4 about; for 5 on; to

5 Broken words

1 dialogue 2 earphones 3 nervous 4 auditions
5 musical

6 Words and phrases

1 getting; ready; for 2 mine 3 worksheet 4 longest
5 label 6 label; largest 7 getting on 8 mean
9 not; as; as 10 than 11 get 12 got 13 Ours; awful

7 The right words

1 very; than 2 as; as 3 long; longer 4 longer; than
5 larger; than 6 not; largest

8 Words and phrases

1 mistake 2 square kilometres 3 tall; big *(oder* large*)*
4 on; Earth 5 about 6 plane 7 read aloud
8 Make sure 9 everything 10 paused 11 scared
12 Punctuation 13 changed

9 Word search

1 means; Scotland 2 aloud 3 mistake 4 scared
5 label 6 plane 7 mine 8 high; worksheet

10 Words and phrases

1 brilliant 2 yours 3 hers; lovely 4 his; even; more
5 most 6 so far 7 on; stage 8 on my own
9 talented 10 cheered; clapped

11 The best words

1 so far 2 even 3 most 4 yours 5 hers

12 Odd one out

1 easy *(keine Qualität)*
2 move *(andere ohne Bewegung)*
3 see *(kein Wasser!)*
4 think *(ohne Geräusch)*
5 question *(andere sind mit „fehlerhaft" verwandt.
Oder vielleicht* wrong, *weil es das einzige Adjektiv ist.)*

13 Words and phrases

1 theatre **2** concert **3** recorder **4** syllables
5 fashion **6** round **7** town hall **8** snow **9** Whose
10 paws; stairs

14 Scrambled story

1 A **2** F **3** D **4** I **5** G **6** E **7** C **8** B **9** H **10** J

15 Words and phrases

1 could **2** clear **3** size **4** correct **5** like this
6 lie **7** are lying **8** wake; up **9** shy

16 Missing words

1 groups; posters **2** Ours; beautiful **3** sure; mistakes
4 text; sentences **5** correct; clear **6** could; better
7 more; colour **8** bit; bigger

17 Words and phrases

1 stuck **2** fork **3** knife **4** spoon **5** drop **6** gel
7 sunglasses **8** glasses **9** arms **10** shake

18 Q & A

1 c **2** e **3** h **4** g **5** a **6** d **7** f **8** b

19 Punctuation

 full stop

 question mark

comma

 exclamation mark

colon

hyphen

20 Words and phrases

1 beeped **2** wish; was **3** stand **4** Most of
5 one by one **6** except **7** good-looking **8** Anyway

21 That's wrong!

1 ~~am~~ → was
2 ~~of~~ streichen
3 ~~geting~~ → getting
4 ~~ring~~ → rang
5 ~~sunglass~~ → sunglasses
6 ~~who~~ → whose
7 ~~any way~~ *(als zwei Wörter)* → anyway *(als eins)*
8 ~~exept~~ → except
9 ~~let fall~~ → drop
10 ~~silbles~~ → syllables
11 ~~artikel~~ → article
12 ~~korrekt~~ → correct
13 ~~claped~~ → clapped
14 ~~nervos~~ → nervous
15 ~~lable~~ → label

Unit 3

1 Words and phrases

1 out and about **2** opposite; post office
3 station; church **4** on the corner **5** cross **6** turn right
7 on the left **8** straight on; past **9** Excuse me
10 tell me the way to **11** ask; the way **12** visitor

2 In town

1 Excuse me, can you help me, please?
2 Sure.
3 Where is the train station?
4 Turn left at the end of the road.
5 I see, left at the end. Right.
6 Then go straight on.
7 Do I cross the road?
8 No, it's on the corner.

3 Words and phrases

1 pedestrian zone **2** after **3** just after **4** cost
5 are closing **6** chocolates **7** need; flowers; stall
8 city **9** plastic; felt pens **10** as; cash desk
11 assistant; set **12** have; got **13** change

4 Broken words

1 pedestrian **2** flowers **3** assistant **4** chocolates
5 change **6** visitors **7** opposite

5 Words and phrases

1 knows about **2** grams; of **3** packets; of
4 tin; of; soup; bottle; of; juice **5** tomato **6** kilos; of
7 plates; of; chips **8** basket; of; fruit **9** sock
10 scan **11** souvenir

6 The right words

1 hungry; packet **2** juice; drink **3** grams; sugar
4 basket; table **5** plate; chips **6** souvenirs; visitors
7 scan; text **8** after; home **9** stalls; market
10 much; kilo

7 Words and phrases

1 magic **2** make **3** fights **4** Just then **5** slowly
6 wall **7** in a loud voice **8** good **9** responsible
10 well **11** Don't worry **12** happened

8 The best word

1 in **2** just **3** good **4** slowly **5** about

9 Opposites

1 open **2** left **3** similar **4** brilliant **5** rainy
6 tall **7** sell **8** object **9** yours

10 Words and phrases

1 describe **2** irregular **3** topic **4** hang **5** highlight
6 underline **7** drafts

11 Scrambled story

1 A **2** D **3** K **4** I **5** G **6** B **7** J **8** L **9** E
10 C **11** H **12** F **13** M

12 Words and phrases

1 broken **2** That's why **3** gate **4** cut
5 cut **6** disappeared **7** down there; up here
8 roof **9** view; of **10** shore

13 Missing words

1 gate; broken **2** why; carefully **3** place; film
4 scene; hid **5** building; quietly **6** Cut; roof
7 view; up **8** fight; lake **9** boat; shore
10 disappeared; ready

14 Words and phrases

1 whisper **2** further **3** hole **4** up to; waist **5** only
6 wood **7** Hurry **8** thanks; to **9** lips **10** hug
11 rescued

15 Scrambled dialogue

1 d **2** c **3** b **4** f **5** a **6** e

16 That's wrong!

1 ~~dissapear~~ → disappear
2 ~~wispered~~ → whispered
3 ~~would~~ → wood
4 ~~slow~~ → slowly
5 ~~desk cash~~ → cash desk
6 ~~Have you a dog?~~ → Have you got …
oder Do you have …
7 ~~costed~~ → cost
8 ~~Hurry on~~ → Hurry up
9 ~~of~~ streichen
10 ~~get~~ → make

17 Word search

1 about **2** broken **3** close **4** cross **5** felt **6** socks
7 highlight **8** underline **9** voice **10** disappear
11 wood **12** shore **13** view

18 -ing words

1 starting **2** interesting **3** whispering **4** closing
5 building **6** working **7** ringing **8** everything
9 good-looking **10** worrying **11** feeling **12** making.
Nicht verwendete Buchstaben: J Q X Z

19 24 x 5

Across: 1 could **3** shake **6** stand **7** round **8** shore
10 alone **11** hurry **14** climb **15** about **16** drama
18 draft **19** torch **20** topic **21** cheer

Down: 2 label **3** stage **4** earth **5** meant **6** stood
8 stuck **9** aloud **12** fight **13** magic **17** after

Unit 4

1 Words and phrases

1 background 2 foreground 3 at the bottom
4 countryside 5 began 6 fields 7 footprints; grass
8 feet 9 mist 10 ponies; valley 11 cows; sheep
12 goats; etc. 13 poem

2 Q & A

1 d 2 e 3 h 4 a 5 c 6 g 7 b 8 f

3 Words and phrases

1 twice 2 once 3 don't; anyone/anybody
4 over there 5 told 6 just 7 I've; made 8 Have; been
9 have; come 10 I've; seen 11 don't; anything
12 anyone/anybody; look around 13 hay 14 key
15 own 16 moor; a; week

4 The right word

1 tell 2 over 3 just 4 looked 5 been 6 anything
7 Everyone 8 Has

5 Words and phrases

1 that way; this way 2 mud 3 leaves 4 leave 5 bath
6 run 7 met 8 brought 9 bought 10 woken up
11 Oh dear; broken

6 That's wrong!

1 ~~brought~~ → bought
2 ~~bathe~~ → bath
3 ~~enything~~ → anything
4 ~~brougt~~ → brought
5 ~~feld~~ → field
6 ~~breaked~~ → broken
7 ~~ran~~ → run
8 ~~hey~~ → hay
9 ~~deer~~ → dear
10 ~~woken~~ → woke

7 Words and phrases

1 lambs; barn 2 bacon; eggs 3 glass; of
4 angry; badly 5 delicious 6 been; to 7 yet
8 I'd love to 9 dirty; pair; of; boots 10 lost
11 strong 12 anything 13 sweet 14 heavy
15 one; more; quick 16 is; missing

8 Broken words

1 delicious 2 Quick 3 badly 4 missing 5 bacon
6 boots; dirty 7 angry 8 heavy

9 Words and phrases

1 chosen 2 drunk 3 found 4 heard 5 read
6 ridden 7 slept 8 marked; up 9 decide
10 interested; in; waterfalls 11 train; takes 12 stamps

10 A scrambled letter

1 A 2 E 3 H 4 F 5 C 6 G 7 B 8 D 9 I
10 K 11 J

11 Words and phrases

1 everywhere 2 for ever 3 for miles 4 hurt
5 can't; any more 6 across 7 impossible 8 passes
9 path 10 raincoat 11 until 12 cried 13 cry

12 Scrambled sentences

1 It's a good idea to take your raincoat.
2 The farmer walked across the valley.
3 It's delicious but I can't eat any more.
4 We walked for miles and my feet hurt.
5 I looked everywhere but didn't find it.
6 Dad said I can't go out until Saturday.
7 We passed nobody on the moor.
8 We rode our bikes on the path.
9 It's impossible to speak ten languages.
10 It hurt when she fell but she didn't cry.

13 Words and phrases

1 jigsaw 2 verse 3 otters 4 trains 5 deer 6 adder
7 tulips 8 adventure 9 nodded 10 wandered
11 cocoa

14 True or false?

1 True
2 False (You nod your head when you think someone
is right.)
3 True
4 False (Tulips are flowers. You can't eat them.)
5 False (When you wander around a place,
you walk slowly.)
6 True
7 False (Cocoa is something that you drink.)
8 False (We say "one footprint, two footprints".)
9 True
10 True

15 Words and phrases

1 both **2** fireplace **3** mug; of **4** ruin **5** ground
6 pretty **7** cottage **8** full of **9** One night
10 believe **11** kind

16 Word search

1 cottage **2** pretty **3** ruin **4** mug **5** ground
6 Both **7** cry **8** full
Lösungssatz: This was fun.

17 Words and phrases

1 closely **2** honour **3** nearby **4** is; moving; into
5 instead **6** don't; either **7** fence; around **8** grow
9 plant **10** didn't; even **11** graves **12** appear

18 Missing pairs

1 closely; see **2** grow; own **3** fence; garden
4 leaving; moving **5** warm; fireplace **6** believe; ghosts
7 lambs; moor **8** once; twice **9** way; minutes
10 pair; boots

Unit 5

1 Words and phrases

1 celebrate **2** celebration **3** parade **4** mayor
5 New Year's Eve; fireworks **6** firework
7 lit; candles; blew; out **8** dressed; up **9** costume
10 special

2 That's wrong!

1 special **2** New Year's Eve **3** favourite
4 *Der Satz ist richtig.* **5** fireworks **6** mayor **7** costume
8 candle **9** blew **10** *Der Satz ist richtig.*

3 Words and phrases

1 buckets **2** crowd **3** festival **4** flags **5** raise; money
6 charity **7** took; part; in **8** planned **9** theme

4 Broken words

1 theme **2** buckets **3** money **4** charity
5 flags; festival **6** crowd **7** planned **8** light

5 Very irregular!

1 blew **2** choose **3** eaten **4** lit **5** taken

6 Words and phrases

1 juggler; juggling **2** drive **3** got out
4 put on **5** took; off **6** pair of gloves; pullover
7 Are; trousers; They're **8** choir; not; till
9 probably; artist **10** torch **11** passed; around
12 Encore **13** promised

7 Match the two parts

1 e **2** h **3** i **4** j **5** d **6** a **7** c **8** b **9** g **10** f

8 Words and phrases

1 journey **2** Queen **3** translate **4** take notes
5 symbols **6** Abbreviations; e. g. **7** at least
8 director **9** than; ever **10** demonstration **11** you see
12 offered Indian **13** lift **14** event; storm

9 The right word

1 of **2** in **3** out **4** for **5** than **6** till

10 Words and phrases

1 million **2** fly **3** flew **4** flown **5** present
6 presentation **7** introduce

11 Scrambled presentation

1 A **2** G **3** O **4** B **5** J **6** F **7** H **8** N **9** L
10 K **11** C **12** M **13** I **14** E **15** P

12 Words and phrases

1 speech **2** competition **3** workshop
4 painted; Spanish **5** main **6** tasty; traditional
7 repeat **8** tongue-twister **9** puppets

13 True or false?

1 False *(A tongue-twister is a sentence or phrase that is difficult to say.)*
2 False *(We use abbreviations when we want to make the word short.)*
3 True
4 False *(If you say something is tasty, it is yummy or delicious.)*
5 True
6 False *(A presentation is the longer than an introduction.)*
7 True
8 True
9 False *(You put on clothes in the morning and take them off at night.)*
10 True

14 Words and phrases

1 have a quick word with **2** famous; for **3** defended
4 invade **5** attack **6** destroyed **7** knight **8** became
9 forgotten **10** given **11** recipe

15 Scrambled questions

1 Have you given anything to a friend this year?
2 What is the area where you live famous for?
3 Do you often forget things?
4 Do you know any good recipes?
5 Have you ever taken part in a competition?
6 When was the last time you saw fireworks?

16 Words and phrases

1 pick up; rubbish **2** picked; up **3** is made of
4 mirror; teeth **5** thunder **6** even if
7 bowl air **8** painted **9** asked; for **10** heart; audience
11 deep; breath **12** paid for **13** chorus
14 lightning; heavy; rain **15** bow

17 Where do the words go?

1 b **2** d **3** b **4** d **5** c **6** c **7** a **8** b

18 Words and phrases

1 interrupt **2** pour **3** circle **4** ring **5** shoulders
6 lit up **7** whistled **8** whole **9** entry **10** conversation

19 Word search

1 pour **2** whole **3** whistled **4** lit **5** entry **6** interrupt
7 ring **8** heavy **9** teeth **10** word

Unit 6

1 Words and phrases

1 cliff; cave **2** bridge **3** real **4** entered; guide
5 each; copy **6** needn't **7** mustn't **8** hand in
9 built; narrow **10** guard **11** legend; king
12 wrote down **13** courtyard **14** prince; princess

2 Match the sentences

1 c **2** h **3** f **4** g **5** a **6** d **7** b **8** e

3 Words and phrases

1 what's wrong with **2** sweets; at Grandpa's
3 while; tapped **4** turned to **5** Stop it **6** hissed

4 Scrambled words

1 wrong; today **2** view; cliff **3** while; watched
4 dogs; hiss **5** each; write **6** tapped; shoulder
7 needn't; hand **8** turned; stop

5 Missing letters

1 king; prince
2 late; parade; every
3 castle; it; celebration
4 the; fireworks; the
5 event; raised; charity
Das Gebäude heißt: Tintagel Castle

6 Words and phrases

1 scream **2** kill **3** groan **4** stomach **5** ill
6 sick **7** be sick **8** well **9** seat **10** reason

7 Match the lines

1 d **2** g **3** k **4** h **5** j **6** c **7** a **8** l **9** f **10** i
11 b **12** e

8 Words and phrases

1 tunnel **2** sticky **3** apple **4** back **5** chest
6 fingers **7** knee **8** neck **9** throat **10** toes
11 tongue

9 Odd one out

1 nose: you only have one
2 heart: you can't move it *oder* it's inside you
3 sing: it's nice
4 shirts: they aren't always in pairs

10 Opposites

1 toes 2 back 3 well 4 queen 5 stop 6 drink
7 narrow 8 village 9 run 10 sticky 11 whisper
12 daughter 13 brilliant 14 take

11 Words and phrases

1 toothache 2 headaches 3 a; temperature
4 cough; sore throat 5 sore 6 has; a; cold
7 plaster 8 thermometer 9 fresh 10 dentist
11 hospital 12 terrible

12 Broken words

1 thermometer 2 temperature 3 sweets 4 sick
5 headache 6 screaming 7 throat 8 cough
9 hospital

13 Words and phrases

1 floor 2 report; strawberry 3 frowned 4 go; red
5 went; mad 6 gone; hard 7 role 8 as 9 as; a
10 Dear 11 melt 12 royal

14 Climb the ladder

6 as 5 melts 4 way 3 went 2 role 1 dear
Das versteckte Wort lautet: dreams

15 Words and phrases

1 consonants 2 vowels 3 noisy 4 peaceful
5 takeaway 6 which one 7 the ones
8 I'll have; vegetarian 9 What size

16 True or false?

1 True
2 False (*They don't eat meat.*)
3 True
4 False (*They are red.*)
5 True
6 False (*They smile.*)
7 False (*It's bad for you.*)
8 True
9 True
10 False (*It's part of your neck.*)

17 Words and phrases

1 stone 2 cast 3 beard 4 adopted 5 Battle
6 enemies; danger 7 truth 8 kiss 9 knelt
10 crown 11 wise

18 Double trouble

1 enemies 2 terrible 3 kis 4 tunnel 5 consonants
6 tapping 7 strawberry 8 coffee 9 toothache
10 apple

19 Sssss

1 son 2 say 3 sweets 4 shout 5 stomach 6 stars
7 stones 8 standing 9 sizes 10 sore 11 stop
12 strawberry

20 What am I?

1 castle 2 wind 3 knee 4 legend

21 Crossword puzzle

Across: 1 voice **3** moon **5** mad **6** tree **11** son
12 million **14** entry **15** copy **16** ago **18** win
19 hard **20** conversation **22** toes **24** enter **26** die
28 yesterday **29** week **30** sit **32** vegetarians
35 claps **36** end **37** ingredients **41** tongue
42 abbreviation

Down: 2 encore **4** barn **7** role **8** torch **9** flag
10 strawberry **12** mayor **13** ill **17** own **19** hat
20 crowd **21** sweets **23** see **25** grave **27** decide
30 shake **31** bridge **33** tap **34** taken **35** costume
38 nod **39** event

3 Words and phrases ➜ (p. 68)

1 We went to the cinema _____ last week.	Wir sind letzte Woche **zweimal** ins Kino gegangen.
2 – Really? I only went _____ last year.	– Echt? Ich bin letztes Jahr nur **einmal** gewesen.
3 I _____ know _____ who speaks Chinese.	Ich kenne **niemanden**, der Chinesisch spricht.
4 My house is _____. See?	Mein Haus ist **da drüben**. Siehst du?
5 Remember? I _____ you yesterday.	Weißt du noch? Ich **habe** es dir gestern **erzählt**.
6 The class has _____ started.	Der Unterricht hat **gerade eben** angefangen.
7 _____ _____ some notes.	**Ich habe mir** einige Notizen **gemacht**.
8 You look awful. _____ you _____ ill?	Du siehst schrecklich aus. **Bist** du krank **gewesen**?
9 Our friends _____ _____ to see us.	Unsere Freunde **sind gekommen**, um uns zu besuchen.
10 _____ never _____ that top. Is it new?	**Ich habe** dieses Top noch nie **gesehen**. Ist es neu?
11 I _____ want _____ to eat now, thanks.	Ich will jetzt **nichts** essen, danke.
12 Does _____ want to _____?	Will **jemand** sich **umsehen**?
13 This is _____. It's for the horses.	Das ist **Heu**. Es ist für die Pferde.
14 Where's my _____? I had it 10 minutes ago.	Wo ist mein **Schlüssel**? Ich hatte ihn vor 10 Minuten.
15 Do most families _____ a car?	**Besitzen** die meisten Familien ein Auto?
16 I go to the _____ twice ___ _____.	Ich gehe zweimal **pro Woche** aufs **Hochmoor**.

4 The right word

Wähle das richtige Wort aus, um den Satz zu vervollständigen.

1 I'm sorry, I didn't hear. Can you _____ me again?

2 She lives in that house _____ there.

3 The film has _____ started.

4 It was interesting when we _____ around the farm.

5 Where have you _____? I was worried.

6 I'm hungry! I haven't eaten _____ all day.

7 Plymouth is in England. _____ knows that.

8 _____ John gone, or is he still here?

1 say · tell · explain · speak

2 by · up · over · next to

3 yet · now · so · just

4 visited · looked · came · saw

5 be · being · been · were

6 anything · something · nothing

7 someone · everyone · anyone

8 have · is · has · was

5 Words and phrases ➡ (pp. 69–70)

1 The school isn't _____ . It's _____ .   Die Schule ist nicht **dort entlang**. Sie ist **hier entlang**.

2 Don't walk in the _____!   Lauf nicht im **Schlamm**!

3 Hurry, the bus _____ in three minutes.   Beeil dich. Der Bus **fährt** in drei Minuten ab.

4 Please _____ some juice for me.   **Lass** mir bitte ein bisschen Saft **übrig**.

5 You need to have a _____ .   Du brauchst ein **Bad** zu nehmen.

6 You've _____ through a lot of mud!   Du bist durch viel Schlamm **gelaufen**.

7 Have you _____ our new neighbours?   Hast du unsere neuen Nachbarn **kennengelernt**?

8 I've _____ you some biscuits.   Ich habe dir ein paar Kekse **mitgebracht**.

9 I haven't _____ anything this week.   Ich habe diese Woche nichts **gekauft**.

10 He's just _____ .   Er ist eben **aufgewacht**.

11 _____! I've _____ the plate.   **Oje**! Ich habe den Teller **zerbrochen**.

6 That's wrong!

Finde und korrigiere den Fehler in jedem Satz.

1 Look at this. I brought it in the new shop.   _____

2 You're very dirty. Go and have a bathe.   _____

3 I don't know enything about Delhi.   _____

4 Here, I've brougt you something to drink.   _____

5 There are lots of animals in the feld.   _____

6 I'm very sorry. I've breaked your pencil.   _____

7 The horses have ran a lot today.   _____

8 I know cows eat grass, but do they also eat hey?   _____

9 Oh deer, I'm sorry but I can't help you.   _____

10 This morning I woken up very early.   _____

7 Words and phrases → (p. 72)

1 The _____ are in the _____. It's warm there.	Die **Lämmer** sind in der **Scheune**. Da ist es warm.
2 I had _____ and _____ for breakfast.	Ich aß zum Frühstück **Schinkenspeck** und **Eier**.
3 Could I have a _____ _____ water, please?	Könnte ich bitte ein **Glas** Wasser haben?
4 I'm _____ when we play _____.	Ich bin **wütend**, wenn wir **schlecht** spielen.
5 "That looks _____," he said happily.	„Das sieht **lecker** aus," sagte er glücklich.
6 Have you ever _____ _____ New Orleans?	**Warst** du schon mal **in** New Orleans?
7 Has your cousin arrived _____?	Ist dein Cousin **schon** angekommen?
8 _____ meet him.	**Ich würde** ihn **sehr gern** kennenlernen.
9 That's a very _____ _____ ____ _____.	Das ist ein sehr **schmutziges Paar Stiefel**!
10 I've _____ my camera. Where is it?	Ich habe meinen Fotoapparat **verloren**. Wo ist er?
11 The ponies on the moor are very _____.	Die Ponys auf dem Moor sind sehr **stark**.
12 "Do you know _____ about lambs?"	„Weißt du **etwas** über Lämmer?"
13 – "Yes, they're _____!"	– „Ja, sie sind **süß**!"
14 Do you need some help? The bag looks _____.	Brauchst du Hilfe? Die Tasche sieht **schwer** aus.
15 I need to make _____ _____ phone call.	Ich muss **schnell noch einen** Anruf machen.
16 Oh no, my phone ____ _____.	Ach nein, mein Handy **fehlt**.

8 Broken words

Bilde Wörter, indem du die Teile miteinander verbindest, und vervollständige die Sätze.

1 The food here is really _____.

2 Look at that! _____, take a photo.

3 They behaved very _____.

4 Not everyone is here. Who's _____?

5 We don't often have _____ for breakfast.

6 You've been in the mud. Your _____ are _____.

7 She was _____ because I broke her camera.

8 It's not a problem, your bag isn't very _____.

y
ous
an
di
he
bo
mis
bac
avy
ots
ba
gry
ick
del
rty
qu
ici
sing
dl
on

9 Words and phrases → *(pp. 73–75)*

1 Have you _____ something to eat? | Hast du etwas zum Essen **ausgewählt**?

2 He can't do anything before he's _____ his tea. | Er kann nichts tun, bevor er seinen Tee **getrunken** hat.

3 I think I've _____ the answer: Tintagel! | Ich glaube, ich habe die Lösung **gefunden**: Tintagel!

4 I've never _____ of that place. | Ich habe von dem Ort nie **gehört**.

5 Haven't you _____ about it in the newspaper? | Hast du nicht in der Zeitung davon **gelesen**?

6 We've _____ there on our bikes before. | Wir sind schon mal dahin mit dem Rad **gefahren**.

7 I've _____ outside before. | Ich habe schon mal draußen **geschlafen**.

8 We _____ _____ the text in class. | Wir haben im Unterricht den Text **markiert**.

9 I can't _____ what I want to do. | Ich kann **mich** nicht **entscheiden**, was ich tun will.

10 Are you _____ ____ _____ ? | **Interessierst** du **dich für Wasserfälle**?

11 The _____ _____ about 20 minutes from here. | Der **Zug braucht** ungefähr 20 Minuten von hier.

12 I have lots of _____ in my book. | Ich habe viele **Stempel** in meinem Heft.

10 A scrambled letter

Verbinde die Texte **A** (Anfang) bis **J** so, dass sie den Text einer E-Mail ergeben.

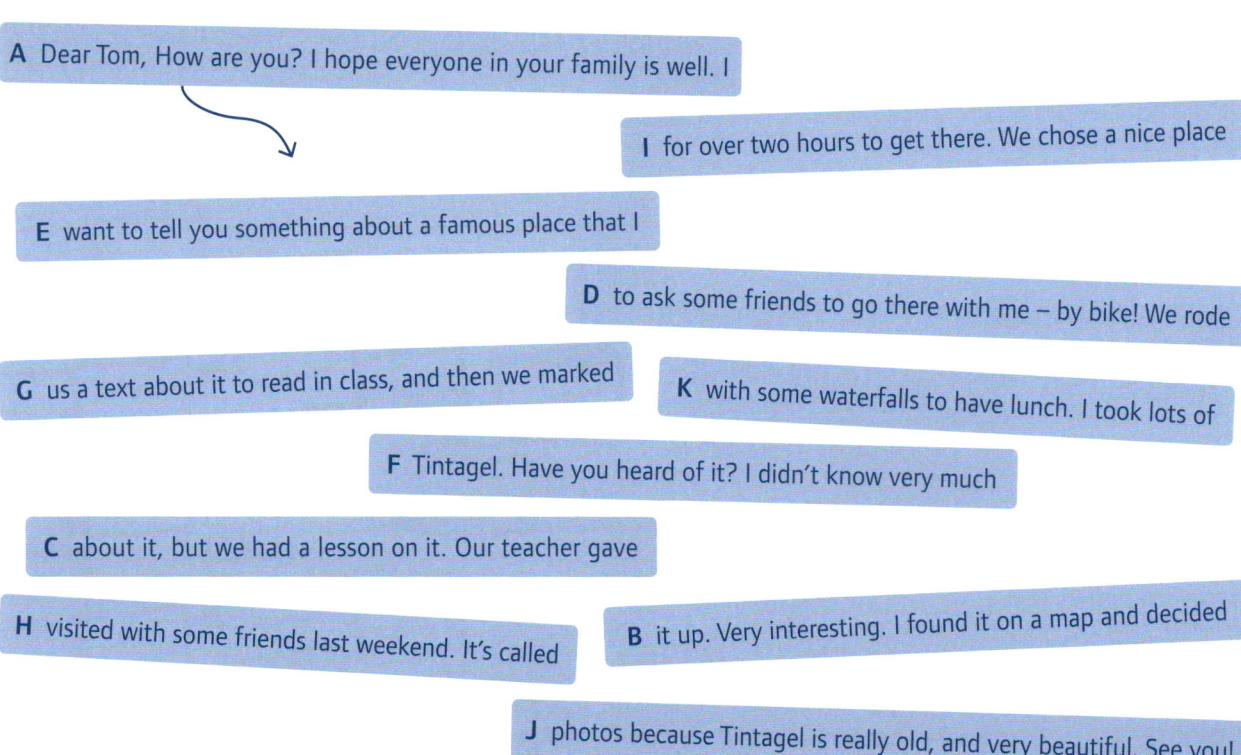

A Dear Tom, How are you? I hope everyone in your family is well. I

I for over two hours to get there. We chose a nice place

E want to tell you something about a famous place that I

D to ask some friends to go there with me – by bike! We rode

G us a text about it to read in class, and then we marked

K with some waterfalls to have lunch. I took lots of

F Tintagel. Have you heard of it? I didn't know very much

C about it, but we had a lesson on it. Our teacher gave

H visited with some friends last weekend. It's called

B it up. Very interesting. I found it on a map and decided

J photos because Tintagel is really old, and very beautiful. See you!

Answer: A ⬡ ⬡ ⬡ ⬡ ⬡ ⬡ ⬡ ⬡ J

11 Words and phrases ➜ (p. 76)

1 There are animals _____ on the farm.	Es sind Tiere **überall** auf dem Bauernhof.
2 I'd like to stay here _____. It's so nice.	Ich würde gerne **für immer** hier bleiben. Es ist so schön.
3 We can see _____ on a good day.	Wir können an einem schönen Tag **meilenweit** sehen.
4 I'm tired and my feet _____.	Ich bin müde und meine Füße **tun** mir **weh**.
5 I _____ walk _____.	Ich **kann nicht mehr** laufen.
6 We walked _____ the moor.	Wir sind **quer über** das Moor gelaufen.
7 Nothing is _____ if you really try.	Nichts ist **unmöglich**, wenn du wirklich versuchst.
8 This bus _____ the school.	Der Bus **fährt an** der Schule **vorbei**.
9 Stay on the _____. It's easier there.	Bleib auf dem **Weg**. Da ist es einfacher.
10 It's raining. Where's my _____?	Es regnet. Wo ist mein **Regenmantel**?
11 Let's stay here _____ the rain stops.	Lass uns hier bleiben, **bis** der Regen aufhört.
12 We heard a young woman. She _____ "Help!"	Wir haben eine junge Frau gehört. Sie **schrie** „Hilfe!"
13 I know it hurts. But try not to _____.	Ich weiß, es tut weh. Aber versuche, nicht zu **weinen**.

12 Scrambled sentences

Schreibe die Wörter in der richtigen Reihenfolge auf.

1 good your a idea to It's raincoat take _____

2 across The valley walked farmer the _____

3 I any more delicious but can't eat It's _____

4 for feet my hurt walked We and miles _____

5 but it didn't everywhere find I looked _____

6 I Saturday out until Dad go can't said _____

7 on We moor nobody the passed _____

8 path our the bikes We on rode _____

9 It's languages speak ten to impossible _____

10 when cry she It didn't but hurt she fell _____

13 Words and phrases ➜ *(pp. 77–80)*

1 I've just finished a big _____ of some horses.	Ich habe eben ein **Puzzle** von Pferden beendet.
2 In class I read a _____ of a poem.	Im Unterricht habe ich eine **Strophe** eines Gedichts gelesen.
3 We saw some _____ in the river.	Wir haben einige **Otter** im Fluss gesehen.
4 Our team _____ every Wednesday evening.	Unsere Mannschaft **trainiert** jeden Mittwochabend.
5 There are hundreds of _____ in the mountains.	Es gibt Hunderte von **Hirschen** in den Bergen.
6 Have you ever seen an _____ ?	Hast du jemals eine **Kreuzotter** gesehen?
7 We have lots of _____ in our garden.	Wir haben viele **Tulpen** im Garten.
8 It was a great _____ yesterday.	Es war gestern ein großartiges **Abenteuer**.
9 I asked, "Are you OK?" He _____ his head.	Ich fragte, „Geht's dir gut?" Er **nickte** mit dem Kopf.
10 I _____ around town for an hour.	Ich **lief** in der Stadt eine Stunde **herum**.
11 I often drink _____ in the evening.	Abends trinke ich oft **Kakao**.

14 True or false?

Welche fünf Sätze sind wahr und welche fünf Sätze sind falsch? Korrigiere die falschen.

	True	False	
1 Otters can swim, but they are not fish.	◯	◯	_____
2 You nod your head when you think someone is wrong.	◯	◯	_____
3 Adders can be dangerous.	◯	◯	_____
4 Tulips are vegetables that you can eat.	◯	◯	_____
5 When you wander around a place, you walk quickly.	◯	◯	_____
6 When something is impossible, you can't do it.	◯	◯	_____
7 Cocoa is something that you eat.	◯	◯	_____
8 We say "one footprint, two feetprints".	◯	◯	_____
9 You hide when you don't want people to find you.	◯	◯	_____
10 A verse is a part of a poem.	◯	◯	_____

15 Words and phrases → (p. 80)

1 I have two cats. I love them _____.	Ich habe zwei Katzen. Ich liebe sie **beide**.
2 My favourite chair is next to the _____.	Mein Lieblingsstuhl steht neben dem **Kamin**.
3 Do you want a _____ _____ cocoa?	Möchtest du ein **Becher** Kakao?
4 Today, the old church is just a beautiful _____.	Die Burg ist heute bloß eine schöne **Ruine**.
5 The _____ is very dry. We need some rain.	Der **Erdboden** ist sehr trocken. Wir brauchen Regen.
6 This is a really _____ village.	Dies ist ein wirklich **hübsches** Dorf.
7 My grandmother lives in an old _____.	Meine Großmutter wohnt in einem alten **Häuschen**.
8 London is _____ interesting buildings.	London ist **voller** interessanter Gebäude.
9 _____ I saw a ghost in my room.	**Eines Nachts** sah ich ein Gespenst in meinem Zimmer.
10 I don't _____ you! There are no ghosts!	Ich **glaube** es dir nicht! Es gibt keine Gespenster!
11 It's important to be _____ to people.	Es ist wichtig, **freundlich** zu Leuten zu sein.

16 Word search

Finde die Wörter im Wortgitter →↓ und vervollständige mit ihnen die Sätze.

1 Have you seen that lovely _____?

2 It's very _____, right?

3 The old castle is a _____ now.

4 I had a _____ of cocoa.

5 Nothing grows in the _____ here.

6 "Do you like dogs or cats?" – "_____."

7 The baby was hungry and started to _____.

8 The city is _____ of tourists in summer.

T	H	I	C	R	Y
S	G	B	O	T	H
P	R	E	T	T	Y
W	O	A	T	R	F
M	U	G	A	U	U
S	N	F	G	I	L
U	D	N	E	N	L

Verwende die übrig gebliebenen Buchstaben aus dem Wortgitter, um einen Satz zu bilden.

17 Words and phrases ➜ (p. 81)

1 Look _____ and you can see fish in the river.	Schau **genau** hin und du kannst Fische im Fluss sehen.
2 It is an _____ for me to be here today.	Es ist mir eine **Ehre**, heute hier zu sein.
3 We ate in a _____ café.	Wir haben in einem **nahegelegenen** Café gegessen.
4 A new family ____ _____ _____ the house.	Eine neue Familie **zieht in** das Haus.
5 He didn't work. He played _____.	Er hat nicht gearbeitet. Er hat **stattdessen** gespielt.
6 I _____ like red and I don't like blue _____.	Ich mag nicht rot und ich mag blau **auch nicht**.
7 There's a _____ _____ the garden.	Es gibt ein **Zaun um** den Garten **herum**.
8 Lots of trees _____ in our garden.	Viele Bäume **wachsen** in unserem Garten.
9 I helped him _____ them.	Ich habe ihm geholfen, sie zu **pflanzen**.
10 I don't like music, _____ _____ pop.	Ich mag keine Musik, **nicht einmal** Popmusik.
11 The _____ around the church are very old.	Die **Gräber** um die Kirche sind sehr alt.
11 Do ghosts _____ there at midnight?	**Erscheinen** dort um Mitternacht Gespenster?

18 Missing pairs

Wer hat die fehlenden Wörter?

1 It's very small, but if you look _____, you can _____ a mouse.

2 We're lucky. We have a garden, so we _____ our _____ vegetables.

3 The deer ate our flowers, so we put a _____ around the _____.

4 My friend is _____ London and _____ to a village.

5 It's nice and _____ by the _____.

6 I don't _____ there are things like _____.

7 We saw a lot of sheep with their _____ on the _____.

8 I've seen the film _____ but I've read the book _____.

9 Let's go this _____. It only takes a few _____.

10 I need to buy a new _____ of _____.

grow own

believe ghosts

fence garden

leaving moving

warm fireplace

closely see

lambs moor

once twice

way minutes

pair boots

Celebrate!

1 Words and phrases → *(pp. 84–85)*

1 How do you _____ birthdays in your family?	Wie **feierst** du Geburtstage in deiner Familie?
2 We went into town to see the _____.	Wir fuhren in die Stadt, um die **Feier** zu sehen.
3 There was a loud _____ through the streets.	Es gab eine laute **Parade** durch die Straßen.
4 We saw the _____ there.	Wir haben die **Bürgermeisterin** da gesehen.
5 On _____ we have _____.	An **Silvester** machen wir **Feuerwerk**.
6 Don't put a _____ in your pocket.	Tu keinen **Feuerwerkskörper** in deine Tasche.
7 I _____ the _____ and _____ them _____.	Ich **zündete** die Kerzen **an** und **pustete** sie **aus**.
8 Last year I _____ _____ as a ghost.	Letztes Jahr **verkleidete** ich **mich** als Gespenst.
9 Everyone said it was a great _____.	Alle sagten, es war eine großartige **Verkleidung**.
10 Do you eat _____ food on New Year's Eve?	Esst ihr **besonderes** Essen an Silvester?

2 That's wrong!

Finde und korrigiere die Fehler. Auf zwei Linien gibt es *keinen* Fehler.

1 Last week was a very spezial week for us because _____

2 we had a New Year Eve party for everyone who lives _____

3 in our town. It's my favorit celebration. _____

4 I like it because there is a parade through the streets _____

5 and at the end we always have firework in the park. _____

6 The major was there last week, and he wore his _____

7 costume with his funny coat and hat. Everyone had _____

8 a candel, and it was very pretty when we all lit them. _____

9 When the music started I blow it out, and then we _____

10 all danced for hours. It was great. _____

3 Words and phrases ➔ *(pp. 84–85)*

1 Lots of people had _____.	Viele Leute hatten **Eimer**.
2 They were in the _____ on the street.	Sie waren in der **Menge** auf der Straße.
3 It was the biggest _____ of the year.	Es war das größte **Fest** des Jahres.
4 There were _____ on lots of the buildings.	Es gab **Fahnen** auf vielen Gebäuden.
5 The people wanted to _____ _____.	Die Leute wollten **Geld sammeln**.
6 The money was for _____.	Das Geld war für **wohltätige Zwecke**.
7 Our school _____ _____ ____ the parade.	Unsere Schule **hat an** der Parade **teilgenommen**.
8 We _____ it for a long time.	Wir **haben** es lange **geplant**.
9 Every year the parade has a special _____.	Jedes Jahr hat die Parade ein besonderes **Thema**.

4 Broken words

Bilde Wörter, indem du die Wortteile miteinander verbindest, und vervollständige die Sätze.

1 My party had a _____: we dressed as monsters.

2 They walk around with _____.

3 They are asking people for _____.

4 It's all for _____.

5 There are _____ in the streets for the _____.

6 A _____ of people watched the parade.

7 I _____ my party for weeks.

8 Dad asked me to _____ the candle.

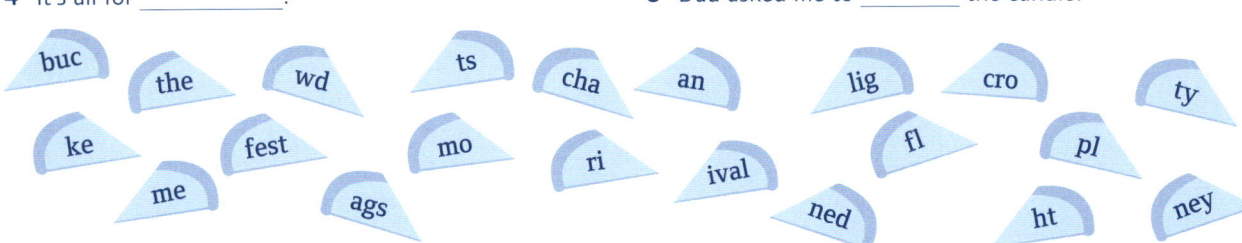

5 Very irregular!

Vervollständige diese Tabelle einiger unregelmäßiger Verben.

1	blow	_____	blown
2	_____	chose	chosen
3	eat	ate	_____
4	light	_____	lit
5	take	took	_____

6 Words and phrases → *(p. 86)*

1 The _____ was _____ balls.	Der **Jongleur jonglierte** mit Bällen.
2 We asked Dad to _____ us into town.	Wir haben Papa gebeten, uns in die Stadt zu **fahren**.
3 We _____ near the cinema.	Wir **sind** in der Nähe des Kinos **ausgestiegen**.
4 I _____ the coat and hat.	Ich **zog** die Jacke **an** und **setzte** den Hut **auf**.
5 Then I _____ them _____.	Dann **habe** ich sie **ausgezogen** und ihn **abgesetzt**.
6 I had a _____ ____ _____ and a _____.	Ich hatte ein **Paar Handschuhe** und einen **Pullover**.
7 _____ your _____ new? _____ nice.	**Ist** deine **Hose** neu? **Sie ist** schön.
8 She's singing in the _____, but _____ _____ 4 pm.	Sie wird im **Chor** singen, aber **erst um** 16 Uhr.
9 You _____ know this street _____.	**Wahrscheinlich** kennst du diesen Straßen**künstler**.
10 He was holding a big _____.	Er hielt eine große **Fackel**.
11 She _____ her holiday photos _____.	Sie **reichte** ihre Urlaubsfotos **herum**.
12 We shouted "_____!" because we wanted more.	Wir schrien „**Zugabe**!", weil wir mehr wollten.
13 He _____ to show us a new trick.	Er **versprach** uns, einen neuen Trick zu zeigen.

7 Match the two parts

Ordne die Sätze 1–10 den richtigen Sätzen a–j zu.

1   My hands are really cold!

2   Your friend is a street artist, right?

3   He's a good singer, isn't he?

4   It's hot in here.

5   I need to go to town.

6   My head is so cold.

7   Don't be late.

8   Are you driving to the centre? Can I come?

9   When does the film finish?

10   Did you like it?

a   Put on your hat.

b   Of course. Get in.

c   OK, I promise.

d   I want to buy some new trousers.

e   Where are my gloves?

f   Yes, I shouted "encore".

g   Not till 11 pm.

h   Yes, he's a juggler.

i   Yes, he's in a choir.

j   Well, take your pullover off.

8 Words and phrases ➜ (pp. 87–92)

1 Did you have a good _____?	Hatten Sie eine gute **Reise**?
2 _____ Victoria was born in 1819 and died in 1901.	**Königin** Victoria wurde 1819 geboren und starb 1901.
3 Don't _____ every word.	**Übersetze** nicht jedes Wort.
4 I _____ because it helps me to learn.	Ich **mache mir Notizen**, weil es mir beim Lernen hilft.
5 I use some _____ because it's quicker.	Ich verwende **Symbole**, weil es schneller geht.
6 _____ like " _____ " are short forms.	**Abkürzungen** wie „z. B." sind Kurzformen.
7 I go to the cinema _____ once a month.	Ich gehe **wenigstens** einmal im Monat ins Kino.
8 I think the _____ is really good.	Ich meine, der **Regisseur** ist wirklich gut.
9 More people _____ _____ were at the parade.	Mehr Leute **als je zuvor** waren bei der Parade.
10 I saw a _____ of the new software.	Ich sah mir eine **Vorführung** der neuen Software an.
11 I'm interested in computers, _____.	Ich interessiere mich für Computer, **weißt du**.
12 She _____ us some _____ food.	Sie **hat** uns **indisches** Essen **angeboten**.
13 Dad is looking for a _____ to Berlin.	Papa sucht eine **Mitfahrgelegenheit** nach Berlin.
14 The big _____ of last week was the _____.	Das große **Ereignis** der Woche war das **Gewitter**.

9 The right word

Vervollständige jeden Satz mit dem richtigen Wort.

1 She is wearing a pair _____ gloves.

2 How many people took part _____ the demonstration?

3 Thanks for the lift. I'll get _____ here.

4 I will wait _____ you after the event.

5 The parade was better _____ ever this year.

6 The show doesn't finish _____ ten o'clock.

1 from · of · with

2 at · to · in

3 out · of · from

4 at · for · in

5 that · as · than

6 for · to · till

10 Words and phrases ➔ *(pp. 92–94)*

1 More than ten _____ people live in London.	Mehr als 10 **Millionen** Menschen wohnen in London.
2 People _____ to lots of countries from here.	Leute **fliegen** von hier aus in viele Länder.
3 Last summer we _____ to Spain.	Letzten Sommer **sind** wir nach Spanien **geflogen**.
4 – Really? I've never _____ before.	– Wirklich? Ich bin noch nie **geflogen**.
5 Here's the photo I want to _____ to class.	Hier ist das Foto, das ich der Klasse **präsentieren** will.
6 It's part of my _____ tomorrow.	Es ist Teil meiner **Präsentation** morgen.
7 I'll show it after I _____ the theme.	Ich zeige es, nachdem ich das Thema **vorstelle**.

11 Scrambled presentation

Verbinde die Texte **A** (Anfang) bis **P** (Ende) so, dass sie den Text einer Präsentation ergeben.

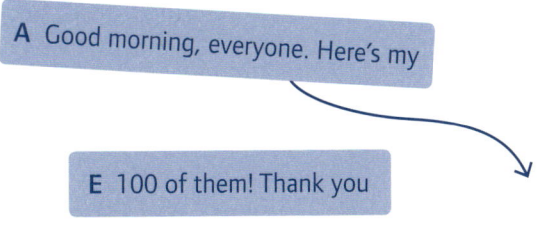

A Good morning, everyone. Here's my

E 100 of them! Thank you

G presentation. The theme I have chosen is "My

C background. I chose this photo because

H my grandmother. It was her 100th birthday, you

O favourite celebration". I have a photo that I

N see! You can see she is in the middle of the

I birthdays, and she has had

D lesson at school. It was in our English

B want to show you to introduce the

F year. It shows my parents, my uncles and

J theme. It's a photo that I took in August last

K uncles, are standing behind her, in the

M it was a very special event. Everyone likes

L photo and her children, my mother and my

P for listening to me. Any questions?

Answer:

12 Words and phrases → *(pp. 94–95)*

1 The mayor gave a _____ about the town.	Der Bürgermeister hielt eine **Rede** über die Stadt.
2 There's a dancing _____ at our school.	An unserer Schule gibt es ein Tanz**wettbewerb**.
3 The poster _____ was cool.	Der Poster**lehrgang** war cool.
4 I _____ some _____ ships on mine.	Ich **habe** einige **spanische** Schiffe auf meins **gemalt**.
5 The _____ thing is a poster is interesting.	Die **Haupt**sache ist, dass ein Poster interessant ist.
6 We tried some _____ _____ food.	Wir haben **leckeres traditionelles** Essen probiert.
7 Can you _____ it? I didn't hear it.	Kannst du es **wiederholen**? Ich habe es nicht gehört.
8 That _____ is impossible!	Dieser **Zungenbrecher** ist unmöglich!
9 When I was little, I had lots of _____.	Als ich klein war, hatte ich viele **Marionetten**.

13 True or false?

Welche fünf Sätze sind wahr und welche fünf Sätze sind falsch? Korrigiere die falschen.

	True	False	
1 A tongue-twister is a word that is difficult to say.	◯	◯	_____
2 We use abbreviations when we can't spell a word.	◯	◯	_____
3 If you repeat something, you say it again.	◯	◯	_____
4 If you say something is tasty, you mean you don't like it.	◯	◯	_____
5 A torch can help you see better when it is dark.	◯	◯	_____
6 A presentation is the same as an introduction.	◯	◯	_____
7 When you have lots of thunder and lightning, it's a storm.	◯	◯	_____
8 If someone offers you a lift, they will drive you somewhere.	◯	◯	_____
9 You put things off in the morning and take them on at night.	◯	◯	_____
10 A parade is an event where people walk in the streets.	◯	◯	_____

14 Words and phrases ➜ (p. 95)

1 _____ we _____ you?	**Dürfen** wir Sie **kurz sprechen**?
2 This area is _____ _____ its beaches.	Diese Gegend ist **berühmt für** ihre Strände.
3 Drake _____ England against the Spanish.	Drake **verteidigte** England gegen die Spanier.
4 They wanted to _____ the country.	Sie wollten **in** das Land **einmarschieren**.
5 They planned to _____ London, I think.	Sie planten, London **anzugreifen**, glaube ich.
6 But Drake _____ their ships.	Aber Drake **zerstörte** ihre Schiffe.
7 The Queen made him a _____.	Die Königin schlug ihn zum **Ritter**.
8 That's why he _____ famous.	Deswegen **wurde** er so berühmt.
9 I've _____ what happened next.	Ich habe **vergessen**, was als Nächstes passierte.
10 My mum has _____ me a nice book:	Meine Mutter hat mir ein schönes Buch **gegeben**:
11 In it there's a _____ from the 16th century!	Darin gibt es ein **Rezept** aus dem 16. Jahrhundert!

15 Scrambled questions

Bilde Fragen, indem du die Wörter in der richtigen Reihenfolge aufschreibst.
Dann beantworte die Fragen.

1 this anything you a year given to Have friend ?

_____ _____

2 you area for live is What famous the where ?

_____ _____

3 often things Do forget you ?

_____ _____

4 good you recipes Do any know ?

_____ _____

5 in Have competition taken you part a ever ?

_____ _____

6 the fireworks When saw time was you last ?

_____ _____

16 Words and phrases ➜ *(pp. 94–95)*

1 Can you _____ that _____, please? | Kann du den **Abfall** bitte **aufheben**?

2 Mum _____ me _____ from school yesterday. | Mutti **hat** mich gestern von der Schule **abgeholt**.

3 Careful, it _____ glass! | Vorsichtig – es **ist aus** Glas.

4 He looked in a _____ and cleaned his _____. | Er schaute in einen **Spiegel** und putzte sich die **Zähne**.

5 I don't like _____. It's scary for me. | Ich mag **Donner** nicht. Er ist mir unheimlich.

6 I want to play football, _____ it rains. | Ich will Fußball spielen, **selbst wenn** es regnet.

7 I had a _____ of soup in the fresh _____. | Ich aß eine **Schüssel** Suppe an der frischen **Luft**.

8 The children all had _____ faces. | Die Kinder hatten alle **bemalte** Gesichter.

9 She _____ _____ help with the show. | Sie **bat um** Hilfe bei der Show.

10 My _____ raced when I saw the _____. | Mein **Herz** raste, als ich das **Publikum** sah.

11 I took a _____ _____ then started. | Ich nahm einen **tiefen Atemzug**.

12 We _____ _____ our tickets and sat down. | Wir **haben** die Karten **bezahlt** und uns hingesetzt.

13 I know the _____ of this song. It's great. | Ich kenne den **Refrain** dieses Liedes. Er ist großartig.

14 There was _____ and _____ _____. | Es gab **Blitz** und **starken Regen**.

15 When you meet the Queen, do you have to _____? | Musst du **dich verbeugen**, wenn du die Königin triffst?

17 Where do the words go?

Vervollständige die Sätze, indem du das entsprechende Wort aus dem Kasten an der richtige Lücke a–d einsetzt.

> **1** doesn't · **2** of · **3** what · **4** the · **5** me · **6** if · **7** a · **8** than

1 a) _____ Rocky, our dog, b) _____ like it when c) _____ there is thunder d) _____ and lightning.

2 All a) _____ I had for b) _____ lunch was a c) _____ bowl d) _____ soup.

3 a) _____ I've forgotten b) _____ they call c) _____ their traditional food d) _____ .

4 This a) _____ traditional b) _____ food is really c) _____ delicious. Can I have d) _____ recipe?

5 a) _____ Mum and b) _____ Dad picked c) _____ up after the d) _____ concert on Saturday.

6 a) _____ I don't want to go to the event b) _____ even c) _____ it doesn't cost d) _____ any money.

7 Drake became a) _____ knight after b) _____ the Spanish c) _____ tried to invade d) _____ England.

8 The parade a) _____ was better b) _____ before because there c) _____ were d) _____ millions of people.

18 Words and phrases → (p. 99)

1 You shouldn't _____ when I'm talking.		Du solltest nicht **unterbrechen**, wenn ich spreche.
2 Can you _____ some water into my glass, please?		Kannst du etwas Wasser in mein Glas **gießen**, bitte?
3 He asked us to stand in a _____.		Er hat uns gebeten, im **Kreis** zu stehen.
4 John has given his girlfriend a _____!		John hat seiner Freundin einen **Ring** geschenkt!
5 I walked 2 km with my cousin on my _____.		Ich lief 2 km mit meiner Cousine auf meinen **Schultern**.
6 The sun _____ everything in the garden.		Die Sonne **hat** alles im Garten **erhellt**.
7 Some people _____ at the end of the show.		Einige Leute **haben** am Ende der Show **gepfiffen**.
8 The _____ day was fantastic. I had fun.		Der **ganze** Tag war fantastisch. Ich hatte Spaß.
9 I'm writing an _____ in my diary about it.		Ich schreibe einen **Eintrag** in meinem Tagebuch darüber.
10 We had a _____ together.		Wir hatten zusammen ein **Gespräch**.

19 Word search

Finde die Wörter im Wortgitter →↓ und vervollständige die Sätze mit ihnen.

1 I started to _____ a drink for her.

2 I spent the _____ weekend in bed.

3 We all _____ when the artist finished.

4 The wonderful fireworks _____ up the sky.

5 I haven't written my diary _____ for today.

6 Please don't _____ me when I'm talking.

7 She has a _____ on her finger.

8 The rain was really _____.

9 Brush your _____ before you go to bed.

10 Can I have a _____ with you, please?

C	X	P	K	T	I
W	H	O	L	E	N
H	E	U	S	E	T
I	A	R	L	T	E
S	V	A	S	H	R
T	Y	L	D	E	R
L	R	I	N	G	U
E	N	T	R	Y	P
D	W	O	R	D	T

A class trip

1 Words and phrases → *(pp. 102–104)*

1 At the bottom of the _____ there's a scary _____.   Am unteren Ende der **Klippe** ist eine gruselige **Höhle**.

2 We walked across the _____.   Wir sind über die **Brücke** gegangen.

3 The man isn't a _____ knight: he's an actor.   Der Mann ist kein **echter** Ritter: Er ist ein Schauspieler.

4 The woman who _____ was our _____.   Die Frau, die **eintrat**, war unsere **Fremdenführerin**.

5 She gave _____ of us a _____ of a map.   Sie gab **jedem** von uns eine **Kopie** einer Landkarte.

6 We're OK. You _____ pick us up.   Uns geht's gut. Du **musst** uns **nicht** abholen.

7 You _____ run. It's dangerous.   Du **darfst nicht** rennen. Es ist gefährlich.

8 You must _____ your homework on Monday.   Ihr müsst eure Hausaufgaben am Montag **einreichen**.

9 The road that they _____ is very _____.   Die Straße, die sie **gebaut haben**, ist sehr **schmal**.

10 A _____ waited for us on the bridge.   Ein **Wachposten** wartete auf der Brücke auf uns.

11 The _____ talks about a great _____.   Die **Legende** erzählt von einem großen **König**.

12 I _____ the information in my book.   Ich **schrieb** die Informationen in meinem Heft **auf**.

13 We took some photos in the _____.   Wir haben ein paar Fotos im **Innenhof** gemacht.

14 The _____ and _____ lived here.   Der **Prinz** und die **Prinzessin** wohnten hier.

2 Match the sentences

Bilde Mini-Dialoge, indem du die Sätze **1–8** den Sätzen **a–h** zuordnest.

1 This is important.

2 I don't think it's a true story.

3 Who is that with the tourists?

4 Is that a real castle?

5 It's not a very big cave, is it?

6 How can we cross the river?

7 They've got some great photos.

8 The plan is to meet outside, I think.

a You're right, it's very narrow.

b Yes, I asked for copies.

c Right, I'll write it down.

d There's a bridge over there.

e OK, see you in the courtyard.

f A guide, I think.

g No, they built it for a film.

h You're right: it's a legend.

3 Words and phrases → (p. 105)

1 I know _____ Jack:	Ich weiß, **was mit** Jack **los ist**:
2 He ate too many _____ ____ _____.	Er hat **bei Opa** zu viele **Süßigkeiten** gegessen.
3 _____ I talked, he _____ me on the back.	**Während** ich sprach, **tippte** er mir auf den Rücken.
4 Our teacher _____ us and smiled.	Unsere Lehrerin **wendete sich zu** uns und lächelte.
5 Don't do that. _____ now!	Mach das nicht. **Hör** jetzt **auf**!
6 I heard a snake. It _____.	Ich habe eine Schlange gehört. Sie **hat gezischt**.

4 Scrambled words

In jedem Satz sind die Buchstaben zweier Wörter durcheinandergeraten. Schreibe die Wörter richtig auf.

1 What's orgwn with him taydo?

2 The ewvi is great from the top of the filcf.

3 He ate some sweets hiwle he tadwche television.

4 Sodg don't sihs, they bark.

5 Our teacher asked ehca person to retiw a report.

6 I pdatep him on the horlusde and asked him to be quiet.

7 She said we enden't nhda in our homework till Friday.

8 She rednut to them and asked them to post it.

5 Missing letters

In jeder Zeile fehlt bei zwei oder drei Wörtern ein Buchstabe. Finde die Buchstaben und schreibe sie in einer Reihenfolge auf, die den Namen eines Gebäudes ergibt.

The kin turned to his son, the price, and told him that he

mustn't be ate for the parad that happened evry winter in

the castle becuse it was a very mportant ceebration that

he people enjoyed, with many firework, and that he

even rised a lot of money for harity.

Name of the building: ◯◯◯◯◯◯◯ Ⓛ Ⓒ◯◯◯◯◯

6 Words and phrases → *(p. 105)*

1 When I watch horror films, I always _____.	Wenn ich mir Horrorfilme anschaue, **schreie** ich immer.
2 I don't think I could _____ an animal.	Ich glaube nicht, dass ich ein Tier **töten** könnte.
3 The teacher heard a _____ from the class.	Der Lehrer hörte ein **Stöhnen** in der Klasse.
4 I'm hungry. My _____ is empty!	Ich habe Hunger. Mein **Magen** ist leer!
5 I didn't go to school because I was ____.	Ich war heute nicht in der Schule, weil ich **krank** war.
6 Do you feel _____?	Ist dir **schlecht**?
7 Yes, I think I'm going to _____.	Ja, ich glaube, ich muss **mich übergeben**.
8 Yes, you don't look _____.	Ja, du siehst nicht **gesund** aus.
9 Please stay in your _____ while we are driving.	Bleib bitte auf deinem **Platz**, während wir fahren.
10 There's a good _____ for that: it's dangerous.	Es gibt einen guten **Grund** dafür: Es ist gefährlich.

7 Match the lines

Ordne die Geschichte. Entscheide, wo die Teile von der rechten Seite (a–l) in die linke Seite einzuordnen sind.

1 Last weekend I went to the	**a** and I heard a strange sound
2 because I wanted to see	**b** his head. Was there a ghost in the
3 that it was a scary film with	**c** happening. A few minutes later,
4 one, he screamed because it was	**d** cinema with a few friends
5 he wanted to leave, but he said no,	**e** my seat made the noise when I moved!
6 eyes so that he couldn't see what was	**f** and asked me the reason for my question.
7 the ghosts wanted to kill a family	**g** a film, but one friend didn't know
8 near me. I didn't know what it	**h** a big surprise for him. I asked if
9 if he felt sick. He said he didn't	**i** Then I heard it again. "Is that your
10 "Someone is groaning," I said.	**j** and put his hands in front of his
11 stomach?" I asked. He shook	**k** ghosts, and when we saw the first
12 cinema? Then I found the answer:	**l** was. I turned to my friend and asked

8 Words and phrases ➡ *(pp. 106–108)*

1 I went through a _____ on the way to the beach.	Auf dem Weg zum Strand ging ich durch einen **Tunnel**.
2 The seat was _____ from the sweets.	Der Sitz war **klebrig** von den Süßigkeiten.
3 I sometimes eat an _____ before I go to bed.	Ich esse manchmal einen **Apfel**, bevor ich ins Bett gehe.
4 I usually sleep on my _____.	Ich schlafe normalerweise auf dem **Rücken**.
5 The doctor listened to my _____.	Der Arzt hat meine **Brust** abgehört.
6 His _____ were very cold!	Seine **Finger** waren sehr kalt!
7 I hurt my _____ when we were playing.	Ich habe mir beim Spielen das **Knie** verletzt.
8 Between the head and the shoulders is the _____.	Zwischen Kopf und Schultern ist der **Hals**.
9 Inside the neck is the _____.	Im Hals ist die **Kehle**.
10 The baby has ten fingers and ten _____.	Das Baby hat zehn Finger und zehn **Zehen**.
11 Don't stick your _____ out. It's not nice.	Streck die **Zunge** nicht heraus. Das ist nicht nett.

9 Odd one out

Welches Wort passt nicht zu den anderen? Und warum nicht?

1 arm   leg   eye   hand   nose   _____

2 finger   knee   heart   arm   toe   _____

3 shout   sing   groan   scream   cry   _____

4 gloves   shirts   boots   shoes   glasses   _____

10 Opposites

Vervollständige die Gegenteile.

1 fingers – t____s

2 chest – b____k

3 ill – w____

4 king – q_____

5 start – ____p

6 eat – ____k

7 wide – n_____w

8 city – v_____e

9 walk – r_____

10 silky – s_____y

11 shout – w_____r

12 son – d_____

13 awful – b_____t

14 give – t_____

11 Words and phrases ➜ (p. 108)

1 I don't want to eat. I've got a _____.	Ich will nicht essen. Ich habe **Zahnschmerzen**.
2 I don't often get _____.	Ich bekomme nicht oft **Kopfschmerzen**.
3 You feel hot. Do you have ___ _____?	Du fühlst dich heiß an. Hast du **Fieber**?
4 I've got a bad _____ and a _____.	Ich habe schlimmen **Husten** und **Halsschmerzen**.
5 After the walk, my feet were really _____.	Nach dem Spaziergang waren meine Füße ganz **wund**.
6 She's ill. She _____ ___ _____.	Sie ist krank. Sie **ist erkältet**.
7 If the cut is small, a _____ is enough.	Wenn der Schnitt klein ist, reicht ein **Pflaster**.
8 The _____ shows it's 20°.	Das **Thermometer** zeigt 20° an.
9 You should go outside and get some _____ air.	Du solltest herausgehen und **frische** Luft schnappen.
10 If you've got a toothache, go to the _____.	Wenn du Zahnschmerzen hast, geh zum **Zahnarzt**.
11 My dad's a doctor. He works in a _____.	Mein Vater ist Arzt. Er arbeitet in einem **Krankenhaus**.
12 Something _____ has happened.	Etwas **Schreckliches** ist passiert.

12 Broken words

Bilde Wörter, indem du die Teile miteinander verbindest, und vervollständige den Text.

1 I need a _____

2 because I want to take my _____.

3 I've eaten too many _____

4 so I am feeling a bit _____.

5 I also have a _____

6 because people are _____ outside,

7 and my _____ is sore

8 because of my _____.

9 Perhaps I should go to _____!

si	ee	ugh	ts
per	th	rmo	it
sp	ing	he	er
scre	the	sw	ho
ad	ure	ro	tem
al	ache	met	am
at	co	ck	at

13 Words and phrases ➜ (p. 110)

1 Our flat is on the ninth _____.	Unsere Wohnung ist im neunten **Stock**.
2 I wrote a _____ on _____ farms.	Ich habe einen **Bericht** über **Erdbeer**farmen geschrieben.
3 My teacher _____ when he saw us.	Mein Lehrer **hat die Stirn gerunzelt**, als er uns sah.
4 Some people ____ ____ when they give a speech.	Manche Leute **werden rot**, wenn sie eine Rede halten.
5 The dog _____ _____ when he saw the cat.	Der Hund **wurde verrückt**, als er die Katze sah.
6 The bread isn't fresh: it has _____ _____.	Das Brot ist nicht frisch: es ist **hart geworden**.
7 Which _____ do you want in the play?	Welche **Rolle** im Stück willst du spielen?
8 The teacher chose me ____ the monster.	Die Lehrerin hat mich **als** Monster ausgewählt.
9 My mum works ____ ___ doctor in a hospital.	Meine Mutter arbeitet **als** Ärztin in einem Krankenhaus.
10 She wrote "_____ John" at the start of her email.	Sie schrieb „**Lieber** John" am Anfang ihrer E-Mail.
11 My ice cream started to _____ in the sun.	Mein Eis fing in der Sonne an zu **schmelzen**.
12 The _____ family is often on TV in England.	Die **königliche** Familie ist in England oft im Fernsehen.

14 Climb the ladder

Vervollständige die Leiter und finde das versteckte Wort.

6 My aunt works ___ ____ as teacher.

5 Quick, eat the ice cream before it ____ __ __ __ __.

4 Can you run all the ___ ____ __ to school?

3 I __ ____ ___ red when they asked me that.

2 Which ____ __ __ __ did you have in the play?

1 The first word of a letter is ____ ____.

The word is: ○○○○○○

15 Words and phrases ➜ (pp. 112–113)

1 AEIOU are not _____.	AEIOU sind keine **Konsonanten**.
2 – No, they are _____.	– Nein, sie sind **Vokale**.
3 Everyone was talking. It was _____.	Alle haben geredet. Es war sehr **laut**.
4 Dad's never excited. He's always very _____.	Papa ist nie aufgeregt. Er ist immer sehr **friedlich**.
5 On Friday evenings, we often get a _____.	Freitagabends holen wir oft **Essen zum Mitnehmen**.
6 I want a burger, but I don't know _____.	Ich will einen Hamburger, weiß aber nicht **welchen**.
7 The best burgers are _____ from here.	Die besten Hamburger sind **die** von hier.
8 _____ a _____ burger, please.	**Ich nehme** einen **vegetarischen** Hamburger, bitte.
9 _____ chips would you like with it?	**Welche Größe** Pommes willst du dazu?

16 True or false?

Welche fünf Sätze sind wahr und welche fünf Sätze sind falsch? Korrigiere die falschen.

	True	False	
1 There are more consonants than vowels in English.	◯	◯	_____
2 Vegetarians sometimes eat chicken and lamb.	◯	◯	_____
3 Takeaways are normally cheaper than restaurants.	◯	◯	_____
4 Strawberries are a type of fruit and they are blue.	◯	◯	_____
5 Britain has a royal family.	◯	◯	_____
6 People frown when they are happy.	◯	◯	_____
7 Meat that has gone green is good for you.	◯	◯	_____
8 "Noisy" is another word for "loud".	◯	◯	_____
9 Chocolate melts in the sun.	◯	◯	_____
10 Your throat is part of your chest.	◯	◯	_____

17 Words and phrases ➜ *(pp. 114–115)*

1 I have a _____ in my shoe.	Ich habe einen **Stein** im Schuh.
2 The film has a great _____.	Der Film hat eine großartige **Besetzung**.
3 You're too young to have a _____.	Du bist zu jung, um einen **Bart** zu haben.
4 Jack is my _____ brother.	Jack ist mein **Adoptiv**bruder.
5 The _____ of Waterloo was in 1815.	Die **Schlacht** bei Waterloo war 1815.
6 He has lots of _____. He's in _____.	Er hat viele **Feinde**. Er ist in **Gefahr**.
7 I don't like football. That's the _____.	Ich mag Fußball nicht. Das ist die **Wahrheit**.
8 Do you _____ your parents good night?	**Küsst** du deine Eltern Gute Nacht?
9 The players _____ for the photo.	Die Spieler **haben** für das Foto **gekniet**.
10 The queen doesn't wear her _____ every day.	Die Königin trägt ihre **Krone** nicht jeden Tag.
11 There's often a _____ old man in legends.	In Legenden gibt es oft einen **weisen** alten Mann.

18 Double trouble

In jedem Satz ist ein Buchstabe verdoppelt, wo er einfach sein soll, oder andersherum. Korrigiere die Fehler.

1 Some people have lots of ennemies.   _____

2 I think that is really terible.   _____

3 She gave him a big kis.   _____

4 We drove through the tunel.   _____

5 The letters B and D are consonnants.   _____

6 Stop taping your fingers on the desk.   _____

7 I think that strawbery ice cream is the best.   _____

8 I don't like cofee.   _____

9 You should see a dentist if you've got tothache.   _____

10 I eat an aple every day. It's my favourite fruit.   _____

19 Ssssss

Fülle die Lücken mit Wörtern, die mit S anfangen.

1 The _____ of a king and queen is a prince.

2 If you _____ why someone did something, you tell them the reason.

3 Eating _____ is not good for your teeth.

4 If someone asks you not to _____ they want you to be quiet.

5 When you eat, your food goes into your _____.

6 A film has a good cast when there are lots of film _____ in it.

7 It's difficult to walk when you have _____ in your shoes.

8 If you are kneeling, you are not _____ or lying down.

9 Big and small are different _____.

10 Your throat can get _____ when you talk or sing too much.

11 You say "_____ it" when someone is doing something that you don't like.

12 A _____ is not a vegetable, it's a red fruit and it's delicious!

20 What am I?

Löse diese kniffligen Wortspiele und schreibe das Lösungswort auf.

1 My first letter is in **come** but not in **go**. My second is in **each** but not in **every**.
My third is in **chest** but not in **back**. My fourth is in **tea** but not in **coffee**.
My fifth is in both **late** and **early**. My last letter is not in **fruit** but it is in **vegetables**.
I'm a kind of building.

○○○○○○

2 I move, but I am not a person or an animal. I blow but I don't have a mouth.
You can see me in the trees. I push the clouds in the sky.
I look like **find** but I sound different.

○○○○

3 You have two of me. I move when you walk. I am a rhyme of **me** but not of **I**.
I have four letters, but one of them doesn't make any noise.

○○○○

4 I'm a type of story. My first half is a **part of the body**.
My second half **doesn't begin**. Some people think I'm true, some are not sure.

○○○○○○

21 Crossword

Löse das Kreuzworträtsel auf der nächsten Seite.

Across →

1 She sings well. She has a lovely ⬜ .

3 See picture.

5 She was angry. She went ⬜ .

6 You can climb this.

11 They have one ⬜ and two daughters.

12 a thousand thousands

14 What you write in your diary.

15 This is not a real crown. It's a ⬜ .

16 The film started an hour ⬜ .

18 opposite (*Gegenteil*) of' "lose"

19 Don't eat that bread. It's gone ⬜ .

20 What you have when you talk with a friend.

22 You have these at the end of your feet.

24 the opposite of "go out"

26 opposite of "live"

28 the day before today

29 seven days

30 You ⬜ on a chair.

32 people who don't eat fish and meat

35 The audience does this at the end of a show.

36 the opposite of "start"

37 things you need to make something to eat

40 See picture.

41 a short form, like 'etc' and Oct for October

Down ↓

2 what you shout when you want more from a singer

4 a building where farmers keep things like hay

7 ⬜ = *Rolle*

8 See picture.

9 See picture.

10 See picture.

12 ⬜ = *Bürgermeister/in*

13 I don't feel well. I feel ⬜ .

17 I did it on my ⬜ without help.

19 See picture.

20 lots of people in one place

21 See picture.

23 It's dark. I can't ⬜ .

25 See picture.

27 ⬜ = *sich entscheiden*

30 You do this with your head to say no.

31 See picture.

33 ⬜ = *tippen, klopfen*

34 Look, she's ⬜ some great photos.

35 See picture.

38 You do this with your head to say yes.

39 ⬜ = *Ereignis*